CONFRONTING RACISM AT DUKE UNIVERSITY, 2017-24

The Clash of Expression and Protection in an Elite University

Donald H. Taylor, Jr.

Donald H. Taylor, Jr.

TABLE OF CONTENTS

Acknowledgments
Introduction
Chapter One: Confederates in Paradise
Chapter Two: Are There Limits to Protest as Free Speech?
Chapter Three: Browntown
Chapter Four: Reckoning with myself
Chapter Five: Free Expression v. Protection in a Global University
Chapter Six: How liberal faculty maintain racist systems
Chapter Seven: Talking and Doing
Chapter Eight: Mass Producing DEI Training
Chapter Nine: DEI Round Trip
Chapter Ten: Why Are You So Obsessed With Race?
Works Mentioned

TABLE OF ABBREVIATIONS

AC   Academic Council

GRID Genomics, Race, Identity, Difference

OIE   Office of Institutional Equity

RCT   Randomized Control Trials

SSRI Social Science Research Institute

DEI   Diversity, Equity, and Inclusion

DUMAC Duke University Management Company

JVG   Joe Van Gogh

NC   North Carolina

UNC University of North Carolina

ACKNOWLEDGMENTS

This is a memoir, so I speak only for myself based on my recollection and perspective. However, there are many people who helped me on the journey of writing this book. My wife Martha tolerated me chatting about it, and she listened to it read aloud straight through on a road trip in April, 2025. Duncan Murrell provided great support through discussing ideas and editing a series of earlier writing, some of which became this book. However, he did not edit this version so all errors are mine alone. I sought to publish this with Duke University Press but my proposal last Summer was unsuccessful. They have so many more authors who want to write in their pages than books that they can publish. As I looked at other options, I came to realize that if I wanted to publish the book I wanted to write, and to do so in a timely manner, then I would have to self-publish.

Others who have provided encouragement, and been friends but who bear no responsibility for any errors are Kerry Haynie and Russell Holloway, my best golfing buddies. Karla FC Holloway helped me long ago when she was a Dean and I was an assistant professor and has provided insightful comments on earlier drafts and provided frank feedback at several points that saved me from myself. I also want to thank my parents for support, and especially my dad Hugh Taylor who talked about what UNC Chapel Hill did for him in his life and in doing so, helped set my sights on education. He also paid for me to go to college, which is a gift for which I am forever grateful.

I believe deeply in the value of education and the good of the research university, and Duke University has been an incredible place to work as a faculty member for 28 years. When

DONALD H TAYLOR JR

I was a freshman moving into Winston Dorm at UNC Chapel Hill in August, 1986, I would have said I'd rather starve than work at Duke. I was wrong and Duke is not only a great global university, but first and foremost, a North Carolina success story and a place that I love. "I'm tar heel born, tar heel bread, and when I die I'll be a tar heel dead" just like Washington Duke and his sons James B. Duke and Benjamin N. Duke.

INTRODUCTION

You think you have a memory, but it has you.

JOHN IRVING, A PRAYER FOR OWEN MEANEY

Confronting Racism at Duke University, 2017-24: The Clash of Expression and Protection in an Elite University is my story of serving in two university leadership posts that required me to pay attention to campus issues that I had avoided during my first two decades as a professor. Doing so helped me understand two interconnected realities: that race is the most persistent idea that has shaped my life, from growing up in rural eastern North Carolina to being a leader at an elite university, and that racist incidents disrupt the normal intellectual debate and dialogue of a University campus like nothing else. The word *confronting* in the title signifies a double meaning. This is a memoir of my coming to understand the power of race in my life, including realizing how incomplete was the version of U.S. history I learned in and out of school. The second meaning acknowledges the repetitive nature of high-profile racist events that disrupted the Duke community during the seven-year period recounted, and our efforts to combat them.

The book spans a time when addressing racism in a variety of forms was a central focus of most campus discourse, from the 2017 Unite the Right protests in Charlottesville, Va., to the

Black Lives Matter marches in 2020, to the Spring, 2024 protests and counter protests of the Hamas attack on Southern Israel in October, 2023 and the subsequent Israeli invasion of Gaza. The so-called racial reckoning of summer 2020 and the embrace of Diversity, Equity and Inclusion (DEI) spread from college campuses to the corporate boardroom—as did the inevitable push back that was accelerated by the Supreme Court striking down of the use of race in undergraduate college admissions in June, 2023. The protests and counter protests that erupted after October 7, 2023 produced strange bedfellows in the ebb and flow of the clash of expression and protection on campus.

Conservatives who had long criticized elite higher education for being too liberal, joined with many reliably liberal Jewish voices to decry antisemitism on college campuses at places like Columbia and Harvard. This realignment has lasted into the first few months of Donald Trump's second term, and a federal antisemitism task force is currently targeting universities with loss of federal money if a broad swath of policies are not revised as the administration wishes. What is at stake is literally the clash of expression (First Amendment, academic freedom) and protection (protecting students and others against antisemitism, and all forms of bigotry). However, as I finish this book in April, 2025, a new question has emerged: Can the Trump Administration remake elite universities as they wish, using federal money as a cudgel? Elite higher education has been embroiled by rapid policy changes and disruptions to NIH funding, enforcement of Title 6 and Title 9 on campus and continuing fallout from the campus protests and encampments of the previous academic year. Columbia, Penn, and Harvard have been directly targeted under the guise of addressing anti-semitism, but the Trump Administration's goal is to remake elite higher education as they see fit.

This book is a half century of my life in the making; these simply are the times into which I am publishing it.

The extreme shifts in views of race, racism and what to

do about it from 2017-24 deserve to be memorialized, because much of it feels as if it never happened. And that is the goal for some. President Trump issued an Executive Order on March 31, 2025, to ban "improper, divisive, or anti-American ideology" from all of the Smithsonian museums. Even as rooting out antisemitism is the Trump Administration's stated mechanism for 'reforming' elite universities, the same government is moving to make certain tellings of U.S. history unallowable. My primary hope for the nation *writ large* is that we would learn to talk about race, our history and and our shared future more clearly. Race is not necessarily the most important thing, but it is a part of most important things. I would trade every Diversity, Equity and Inclusion (DEI) training for an honest conversation of our shared history. What is needed is a conversation and no one's indoctrination.

The goal of higher education is to form intellectually resilient citizens who are prepared to pursue their career goals. The most important thing that a professor can provide students is a model for how to debate, and whether (and when, and how) to change one's mind: how to think, not what to think. The best model that society has for how to think are the numerous disciplinary norms that govern how faculty conduct their research. The culture of campus dialogue and debate is broken and needs to be reinvigorated, and I have been thinking and writing about this in some detail on my substack, but not in this volume. My 28 years as a professor at Duke has taught me that nothing more inflames the intellectual debate on campus like a racist event: be it an antisemitic, anti-black, anti-asian, or anti-immigrant attack because such events have at their heart a claim that some people are more valuable than others. This is anathema to the idea of a university, that the search for truth should proceed based on evidence, and not prejudice. I am blessed to have a sabbatical year to think and write at the end of my seven-year administrative and leadership focus and am focusing on higher education reform and how to revitalize the intellectual culture of expression and debate that swirls around and includes undergraduate students. That work builds upon this volume. But first things first. This is my story of confronting Racism at Duke, 2017-24.

CHAPTER ONE: CONFEDERATES IN PARADISE

Begin at the Beginning, the King Said, Very Gravely, and Go on Until You Come to the End: Then Stop

LEWIS CARROLL, ALICE IN WONDERLAND

I sat on the balcony of my hotel room overlooking Waikiki Beach in Honolulu, Hawaii, in August 2017, and talked briefly by telephone with the new president of Duke University, Vince Price, and then with some of his staff. The question at hand was whether Duke should remove a statue of Robert E. Lee from the entrance to the Duke University Chapel. The statue had been defaced the previous evening after the White supremacist marches in Charlottesville, Virginia, and the subsequent murder of a counter-protester. Requests for permits from outside groups to protest on campus had been denied, yet President Price was worried about the possibility of violence. The president consulted me because my term as the elected chair of the Academic Council at the university had just begun, and that position came with the impossible job of "representing" the more than 2,000 faculty at Duke University spread across twelve divisions in ten schools, from the School of Medicine to the School of Divinity.

This elected faculty governance post provides the perspective of a faculty leader and executive committee to the university leadership, as decisions are made and before they are finalized and announced. This system is more than 50 years old and the subtle influence of faculty governance at Duke is unusual, and over time has helped to produce a culture of mutual respect between faculty leaders and the university administration, to the benefit of both. The topics engaged as chair span the mundane and esoteric of academic minutiae to the symbolic, public, and potentially explosive that commonly thrust the university into the headlines of the culture wars. Both President Price and I had assumed our posts just forty-five days before. It was the first crisis for us both, but it would not be the last. The rhythm and focus of the job to come was defined by events outside of my control as chair, both on campus and off.

After the call I returned to the beach and my wife asked what President Price wanted to talk about. When I answered, "Robert E. Lee," she looked puzzled and said, *"What?"*

Indeed.

Decisive Action, Missed Opportunity

President Price made the bold decision to remove the statue. He pledged to use this opportunity to further Duke's research and educational mission, while also taking time to consider how we would do that. The president appointed a Commission on Memory and History, chaired by a faculty member and trustee, to advise him. An email to the Duke community announcing the President's decision had as its header

Statue will be preserved for students to study University's complex past.

The initial group that President Price appointed did not approach the subject as business as usual; they issued clear answers to the questions posed to them in just two months—

a veritable warp speed for a university body. In November 2017, the Commission on Memory and History offered a series of recommendations, including that Duke should leave empty the perch in front of the chapel that had held the statue of General Lee, at least for the time being. As dean of the Chapel, Luke Powery said:

"The gap (in the place where the statue had been) represents a hole in the heart of the United States and the ongoing struggles of racism, hatred, and bigotry—all the things we're seeing in our streets. We haven't come as far as perhaps we thought we had come as a nation."

Michael Schoenfeld, Duke's vice president for communications, said the statue would be safely stored and that the goal was education. "We want people to learn from it [the statue] and study it and the ideas it represents. What happens to it and where it will be is a question for further deliberation."

A second group was charged with developing principles to guide commemorations on campus more broadly, and to codify a process by which Duke would consider requests to rename existing buildings. There was some good initial momentum as a variety of campus committees and groups continued throughout the remainder of the academic year. This work was well-done and needed. For example, Professor of History Thavolia Glymph hosted a conference in March 2018 that considered the history of memorials on college campuses and how universities have discovered and told their own histories. That was an example of the university putting faculty experts to the forefront of difficult issues, and this event demonstrated interest in learning more about Duke's own history as a part of our teaching and research. This idea especially resonated with many in the Duke community, since Robert E. Lee was an icon of the "lost cause" of the Confederacy but had no known connection to Duke University. How and why had he been so memorialized? A key refrain that I heard from a variety of faculty, students, and staff was that what Duke most needed was to learn to talk more about our own history. This very much resonated with me because of my emerging interest in genealogical research and personal readings on North Carolina history, and how incomplete was the version that I had been taught.

However, Duke missed an opportunity to re-purpose the Lee statue as a catalyst for learning and discovery centered on Duke's own campus, history, and role in Durham—the statue remains in its undisclosed location. The earnest commitment to learn and discuss Duke's history waned and had given way to managing the next crisis and to the politics and process of renaming buildings. And it would have been controversial to bring back an icon of the Confederacy, but we had an opportunity to transform a divisive symbol into a shared point of learning and discovery. Duke's Centennial celebration in 2024 did of course focus on our past, but it was a highly curated version as such events are bound to be for large organizations who seek to mass-produce a look back as a catalyst for future fundraising momentum.

Duke University had already renamed a building in June 2014, when the Aycock Residence Hall had its original name of East Residence Hall restored, and the process followed was ad hoc and informal. It was relatively easy to remove Governor Charles B. Aycock's name from a building, due to his history of ideological White supremacy and disenfranchisement of Blacks during his 1900 to 1904 term, since he had no connection to the university and had given no money to it, but there would be more difficult requests. Duke now has a thoughtful process for reconsidering building names that can only be triggered by a written request from within the Duke community. Paradoxically, creating a process for renaming buildings in the future served to make it easier for Duke to sidestep our earlier commitment: to use the Lee statue as a catalyst to look comprehensively at Duke's history. We had elevated the naming/re-naming process that was limited and focused, and this undermined – in time and energy – any effort to create a space dedicated to learning about Duke's history. We lost the catalyst for an ongoing and academic inquiry. What developed was controlled and limited instead of dynamic and expansive because it focused on the naming of buildings.

There was a phrase that Mike Schoenfeld, my friend and former vice president for communications, commonly used when a crisis was quelled, averted, or survived, and the question turned to what to do next. "Let's don't break back into jail," he would say, by which he meant that bold, decisive action in the midst or aftermath of a crisis risked reigniting a controversy or starting a new one. Putting a statue of Robert E. Lee back up in a museum space on campus might be the very definition of breaking into jail, though I think it could be done in a thoughtful way that expanded the on-ramps to discovering Duke's history and talking about what it means for us today.

The locus of energy remained largely reactive. The history department proposed reinstating the original name of "Classroom Building," to the Carr Building, where the department is located on East Campus. This put the president's new process for potential building name changes to immediate use. Julian Carr was an ideological White supremacist, as was Aycock, but he was an industrialist and successful businessman instead of a governor. They were contemporaries, but renaming the Carr Building was more complex since Julian Carr gave the land for what today is Duke's East Campus. This enabled Trinity college to relocate to Durham in 1892, paving the way for the 1924 gift that renamed it Duke University, after James B. Duke's death. Carr's gift was unusual as far as gifts to universities go, in that he appeared to want nothing in return for his generosity. Further, the building in question was named for Carr only after his death. The history department's proposal carefully noted this context in making the renaming request, but it was criticized by some on and off campus.

Criticism on a university campus is to be expected, yet it seemed that some of the most vocal were responding to a nonexistent straw man and not the carefully researched and argued proposal written by a group of history professors. An example of this was a piece written by political columnist Rob Christensen in the Raleigh News and Observer that was unfair because it mischaracterized the proposal that was put forth at Duke. I confirmed by correspondence with Mr. Christensen by email that he had not read the heavily researched and carefully argued proposal before penning his column. He knew the story that he wanted to tell, and Duke seemed to provide the opportunity. This is the reality of a high-profile college campus, where many people seek to use the (in)actions of the university to illustrate what they believe to be self-evidently true.

One aspect of Christensen's criticism turned out to be true. The renaming of the building and the placement of a plaque in the entrance about Julian Carr, and why Duke reinstated the original name, *was* largely the end of the discussion, instead of the beginning of the campus learning more about the relationship of Carr to Duke. The first test of Duke's new renaming policy was orderly and well argued, but it failed to encourage more learning, discussion, and understanding of university history. Instead, it reinforced renaming as the main mode of action. A museum containing the Lee statue as an artifact might have spurred ongoing scholarly discovery and discussion of Duke University's history, but renaming buildings was easier. We should have done both.

On August 16, 2018, President Vince Price announced just before the start of the fall semester that the nave in front of the Duke Chapel where the Lee statue had been would remain empty indefinitely. Price's announcement was timed to set the tone for the academic year:

"There have been many nominations for individuals who should be memorialized by a statue in that space. At the same time, I have heard from a large number of our fellow Duke community members who support extending the Commission's interim recommendation for a longer, even permanent term: that is, to leave the space vacant. As Dean of Duke Chapel and Reverend Luke Powery suggested almost a year ago, the empty space might represent "a hole that is in the heart of the United States of

America, and perhaps in our own human hearts—that hole that is from the sin of racism and hatred of any kind."

I have concluded that Dean Powery's suggestion is the right one, particularly when combined with the placement of a plaque in the foyer of Duke Chapel, which explains why the space is empty. It will provide a powerful statement about the past, the present and our values. I informed the Board of Trustees of my decision this summer, and I received their enthusiastic endorsement of this approach."

The president highlighted three other commitments. The first instructed the president's Arts Advisory Committee to suggest an appropriate way for Duke to honor those people who built Duke University's campus, and the second was to determine how the university could commemorate the first African American students who attended Duke University in the late-1960s. The renaming of Reuben-Cooke Building and the Wall Building was responsive to these commitments. The last recommendation was bolder, and surprised me in a positive way:

"And third, I have asked Executive Vice President Tallman Trask to identify a location on campus where we can mount rotating exhibits dedicated to the history of Duke. As the Commission last fall stated in the principles it set forward to guide us as we think about history and memory at Duke, "The educational mission is central. Therefore, the goal should be to engage with history and never to erase it. The establishment of a living museum will help us fulfill that aspiration on an ongoing basis."

Six years later, no such living museum has been established. Just a few days later, on August 20, 2018, the Confederate memorial on nearby UNC Chapel Hill's campus, euphemistically known as "Silent Sam," was pulled down by a group of protesters while the police pulled back and watched. My thoughts quickly turned to what the destruction of the monument might mean for Duke's plans for commemoration on campus, especially what would become of the Lee statue and the just-promised living museum space. Duke enjoys many more degrees of freedom than UNC Chapel Hill does in dealing with any issue that erupts into the public eye. For example, when the Lee statue was removed from Duke Chapel in the wake of the Charlottesville violence, Duke denied outside groups the opportunity to protest on campus. Public universities do not have that option. Duke had a golden opportunity, which UNC never had, to model how to dialogue about race, racism, and commemoration of our institutional history. The prospects were intellectually exciting, but Duke has only partially embraced this opportunity, and no campus focal point for such an investigation of institutional history and how it affects us today exists on campus as of March 2025. I assume the Lee statue remains in a warehouse somewhere.

The naming of buildings has subsequently figured prominently in campus discussions of racism. In 2022 the social sciences building was renamed for Wilhelmina Reuben-Cooke. Doctor Reuben-Cooke was worthy of commemoration given that she was an educator from a family of educators who was one of the first five Black undergraduate students to attend Duke University. This was a proactive step of the university administration, now following through on their commitment to be mindful of the diversity of people who have figured in Duke's history, a commitment made when announcing the spot in front of the Chapel where the Lee statue had been, would remain empty. In February 2024, the university named the East Campus cafeteria building the George and George-Frank Wall Center for Student Life. George Wall was the first custodian hired by Trinity college, and his son George-Frank Wall worked as a custodian at Duke for fifty years and left $100 for the Duke scholarship fund in his will when he died in 1953, more than a decade before the first Black student or faculty member studied or taught at Duke. Both tributes are well-deserved and broaden the types of Duke community members recognized which was a goal of President Price's, but they do not in themselves represent a vibrant intellectual discovery and discussion of Duke's history. Duke University missed an opportunity to provide more leadership in addressing our own history as scholars, with a goal of normalizing talking about it.

Was Removing Confederate Monuments a Mistake?

The short answer is no, but that depends upon the motivation for the change and the process followed. A mob is not a good process, for example, and that was the way that a Confederate monument near the Courthouse was torn down in Durham, N.C. in August, 2017 after the violence in Charlottesville, Va., and "Silent Sam" was similarly torn down by a mob on UNC Chapel Hill's campus in August, 2018 following months of protest and negotiation regarding its removal. A thoughtful and lawful process should be used to remove monuments, not whatever an angry crowd thinks should be done.

The City of New Orleans had a lengthy, proactive process initiated by their Mayor that resulted in the removal of Confederate monuments in New Orleans, La. in April 2017. The process they used was thoughtful and a model of how such a change should be considered. The history of who was memorialized, when and what was said about it was fully documented and discussed by grounds of historians as well as seeking public comment. Plans for how to remove monuments as well as what to do with them were made ahead of time, and the plans were executed professionally, and in a way that was safe. Such a process could also be undertaken and the decision made not to make any changes. Briefly, here is my reasoning for why the removal of Confederate monuments from public places is a good idea so long as a reasonable process is followed.

First, the Confederacy was a traitorous rebellion against the United States. Military officers fighting for the Confederacy violated their oath to defend and protect the US Constitution. And loyalties to States did not override this responsibility–the point of the Constitutional Convention was to create the United States of America, and to keep the dissolution into individual states as nations that was probably inevitable if we had continued under the Articles of Confederation our first "Constitution."

I do not think that leaders or the cause generally of a traitorous rebellion should be honored with Statues and Monuments in public spaces. If you want to have a Confederate flag on your personal property, that is your choice and right under the 1st Amendment. I don't believe the likes of Jefferson Davis and Robert E. Lee should have ever been honored in public spaces given their role in rebellion against the United States, and the same logic makes it quite reasonable to so remove monuments, change the name of roads, or to rename Military bases if the person so-honored fought against the United States Army in the Civil War. That is, in fact, what every Confederate soldier did, and officers and political leaders such as Jefferson Davis do not deserve continued commemoration in these ways.

I make a distinction between monuments and the like in cemeteries as compared to those in public places. There were two waves of Confederate memorials and monuments in North Carolina. The first occurred in the two decades after the Civil War when statues and monuments were erected in Cemeteries to honor the dead. I think these were and are fine to remain, and defeated people deserve the right to grieve for lost sons, husbands and fathers. The second wave, however, were symbols erected between 1900 and 1930 in opposition to following through on what our nation said we were going to do after the Civil War. They were erected in defiance of the 13th, 14th and 15th Amendments to the U.S. Constitution. *The reason they were erected makes it clearer to me that they should come down.*

There is an excellent multimedia site that documents the two waves of Confederate commemoration in North Carolina that was created by two historians from UNC Chapel Hill, Jim LeLoudis and Cecilia Moore (https://silentsam.online). The site does a good job of providing the context for the role of these monuments in the State's history and is a good example of public history. We need more of this. And I agree with folks who say we do not need to erase history–we need to actually learn and wrestle with it-and not a sanitized or whitewashed version and removing or relocating monuments can and should be a part of this process. Moving monuments to museums is fine, but each statue does not have to be treated as if it were human remains. They are stone and metal. Some of them can just go away. Maybe it is fine to just let Duke's Lee statue collect dust unviewed.

How and who is commemorated on a campus and in a culture are long-standing issues of scholarship, debate, and disagreement. There is far too much heat and not enough light in our present discourse on the topic, and the result is the elevation of naming and renaming events over deep understanding of history and how it affects us today. What we need is to discover our past in a truthful manner and learn how to talk about it. We will not all agree on what the past means for the present and that is fine. In fact, that is the point. Universities should probably be slower to name buildings and the like than we are. Most importantly is this fact that should loom over all such discussions: those we will never meet will someday judge the lives we live today. In what ways will they find our lives to be wanting?

CHAPTER TWO: ARE THERE LIMITS TO PROTEST AS FREE SPEECH?

To sin by silence when they should protest, makes cowards of men

ABRAHAM LINCOLN

I brought an absolute and untested commitment to academic freedom and freedom of speech to my term as Academic Council chair. This was tested on April 11, 2018, when twenty-five undergraduate students rushed the stage in Page Auditorium and shouted down President Price as he began delivering his first alumni weekend keynote address. Some of their demands directly addressed racism and others did not, but the student protesters were a diverse group. After ten minutes of shouting demands through a bullhorn, side negotiations with administrators, and amidst shouting and booing from the mostly White audience, the students left the building and resumed their protest outside, where they further discussed their demands and held a press conference. The president gave his speech and announced class gifts as had been planned, but the event was transformed from a celebration into an intense affair by the protest. Was this simply the exercise of free speech that many say we need more of on campus? Or had a line been crossed? President Price was asked in a Q & A afterward for his thoughts on the protest that had just transpired. He said:

"The challenge now in a culture that confuses shouting back and forth with conversation, we just have to find vehicles to have honest discussion and I'm happy to take up any of the issues which the students raise," he said. "I disagree deeply that this was an appropriate way to handle these issues."

I watched a video of the event and agreed with President Price that the form or method of protest used was inappropriate; it was suppression of speech when the protesters shouted through a bullhorn, "President Price get off the stage." Most of my previous three decades of life had been spent on a college campus as student, post-doctoral fellow or faculty member yet I had not thought much about freedom of speech, academic freedom, nor the role of protest. The role of chair forced me to do so, and it turned out that I was not a free speech absolutist after all, and I told one of the student leaders over breakfast a week later that their tactics had been wrong. I had a visceral reaction to shouting someone down on campus, especially when they were engaging in simply doing their job. We agreed to meet and discuss what had taken place and to see how we might move forward. This first meeting was a bit awkward and tense, but I came to admire this student and his passion. He calmly explained his belief that the university had not been listening to the demands of students, faculty, and staff for years, and that he viewed their protest as linked to the (in)famous Allen Building takeover in 1969. He believed the spring 2018 protest was the continuation of a half-century struggle that he and his group saw as continuing. They felt the need to escalate their tactics, or nothing would be done to address their demands.

This student listened and was thoughtful when I asked him what he would do if a counter-protest group shouted him down at a future event calling for graduate student unionization, or an increase in Duke's minimum wage, or another cause about which he and the group of protesters were passionate. I went on to share with him that I thought their demands were incoherently broad. They ranged from calling for a specific set of punishments for the use of racial slurs on campus, to the banning of circumcision in Duke's health care system. The first is plausibly addressed by the university (though I think it impossible to do well), while the second is not, and there were many policy demands in between. I told him I thought the language of demand was overused and that noise could not substitute for making a persuasive case. He disagreed and explained how the causes were linked and noted that reasonable claims had been made for years and decades on some of the matters. We agreed to remain in communication, and I left with several thoughts. First, it was clear that I was not actually a free speech absolutist and saw limits to protest, which is a form of speech. Second, it was clear that I needed to think more clearly about the concepts of freedom of speech and academic freedom because drawing the line was difficult. I had not spent much time thinking about this, because I had always felt able to speak when I wished. Finally, and most importantly, Duke needed a culture that enabled and encouraged dialogue on a large scale, like the conversations this student and I came to enjoy on a one-to-one basis. This last point was the most important: such dialogue is what Duke needs more of. Creating the culture that we need and want remains a work in progress.

The student shared with me his belief that part of the ferocity of the crowd responding to the protest was because the mostly White crowd saw a racially diverse group of students daring to interrupt their event, and that was unacceptable. I told him that I doubted that was the case, but looking back I am not so sure. The diversity on the stage as compared to the alums sitting in the auditorium is a sign of how much the student body at Duke has changed: in terms of income, race, national origin, religion and certainly the interconnected lives that students lived today are unimaginable when the gathered alums were students.

Graduation was only a few weeks away and the president and his staff were worried that there would be a protest of the commencement ceremony, which I would lead as chair of the Academic Council. Graduation ceremonies have outsized importance on college campuses, not only because they confer degrees, but at Duke summer is a time that provides a paradox. A more relaxing time that is simultaneously more productive in terms of academic output in the form of writing, be it grant applications, articles or books. These are the outputs that faculty most value, and anything other than a successful graduation season portends extra and unwanted work and discussion on topics outside of writing projects interspersed with vacation. That is why the protest threatening to leak into graduation season was viewed as so objectionable to the faculty whose practices set the culture of the University. I enjoyed carrying the mace of the university to lead the faculty procession in ceremonies, but I knew the pomp and circumstance could be upended by a protest, and I was not excited about that possibility. When I saw President Price a few days after the protest for a scheduled meeting, I was struck by how angry he remained. I told him that I agreed, the tactics used were inappropriate, but it was not a personal attack on him, which is how he had experienced it. He was the president, the embodiment of Duke at a point in time, and the university was the target, not Vince Price. The president noted that it was easy for me to say that, since I was not the one shouted down. He argued that the students had violated Duke's policy on protests and pickets, which had been instituted in the aftermath of the 1969 Allen Building takeover. The protest policy was and remains succinct:

"Disruptive picketing, protesting or demonstration on Duke University property or at any place in use for an authorized University purpose is prohibited."

The protest that occurred at the alumni weekend event clearly violated this standard. But the policy seemed overbroad to me, and my first thought was that it was a violation of the

First Amendment, which just showed that I did not understand this bedrock of the Bill of Rights. I had to learn a great deal about this crucial topic that I had previously never had a reason to think about. Freedom of speech is a concept gleaned from five distinct prohibitions in the First Amendment that limit what the government can do to prevent different types of speech:

- According to the First Amendment, Congress cannot pass a law that:
    - Declares a State religion <u>or</u> limits the practice of any religion
    - Limits an individual's freedom to speak
    - Constrains the speech rights of the press
    - Prevents people from peacefully and voluntarily assembling or gathering together
    - Stops people from communicating their displeasure with government policy

Since Duke is a private institution, it is not bound by the First Amendment and therefore can have policies that limit the ability to protest. I thought Duke's policy on protests and pickets was not sufficiently nuanced, but there was no doubt that a private university could legally have this policy. Determining how to enforce it was another matter, and that became the task of the university's Office of Student Affairs after the students disrupted the president.

Academic freedom is not a constitutional right, but a part of an employment contract. Faculty are granted academic freedom to encourage robust intellectual discourse, debate, disagreement, agreement, and the changing of one's mind based on evidence that is consistent with how fields of study decide matters of truth, fact, and beauty. Universities do not have to bestow academic freedom on faculty, but most have chosen to do so. Academic freedom is most clearly secured by the concept of tenure. Not everyone on a college campus has the full protection of academic freedom, though a well-functioning university should protect the ability of all people to speak with broad freedom. The ideal campus has robust debate that allows all members of the community (faculty, students, staff), and those from outside in some cases, to debate and consider ideas so long as they take public responsibility for their words. In this way, a modicum of academic freedom is granted to students and others who engage in campus dialogue, but most members of the university community still don't have the full guarantee of academic freedom that faculty do.

I had given more than two decades of my life as a faculty member without thinking closely or clearly about freedom of speech and academic freedom. I simply made assumptions, perhaps because I had never felt my ability to speak had been threatened. Certainly not in my research as a health policy scholar, where the norms of research design, statistical inference and the like governed even the harshest debates with a predictable comity. Even in my side gig of being a health policy blogger during the Obamacare debate I had carved out a niche of having a viewpoint that was tethered by evidence and sought to provide the benefit of the doubt. There had not been any reason for me to think about freedom of speech and academic freedom in the abstract because I could say what I wished, even though my arguments did not always persuade.

When faculty – like me – don't think much about these issues because our speech in our academic discipline is not under threat, then the culture of debate and dialogue on campus is at risk in other ways. For example, the public debate and discussion on campus is now commonly understood to be dysfunctional and I agree. Renewing and reinvigorating a dynamic marketplace of ideas is among the most needed reforms in higher education. I just did not look closely until I pulled up from my own narrow interests, served as a campus leader and had my teaching assignments reoriented toward introductory undergraduate courses and saw how stilted student discourse had become.

As the 2018 academic year wound down, the question of whether the student protesters would be charged with a violation of Duke's community standard became an active question. I had mixed feelings. On the one hand, the protest policy was too broad, and this would seem like retribution. On the other hand, what took place was unambiguously disruptive and that was against Duke's stated policy. The students were not fractionally over the line established by the policy, they blasted right through it. They had been warned in writing before the protest that they were about to violate university policy. And civil disobedience means you are willing to suffer the consequences of your actions to make your point. The reason Martin Luther King Jr.'s "Letter from Birmingham Jail" resonates is because he was writing from jail, having accepted the consequence of his civil disobedience.

But students who felt the university had not done enough to punish people who perpetrated racist incidents on campus in the past asked why the university was considering cracking down on student protesters. The university had long adopted a robust free speech perspective that argued specific penalties for hate speech could not reliably be devised or implemented. When a noose was hung on a tree near the Mary Lou Williams Center for Black Culture, and the student perpetrator later came forward, they were not punished because they claimed to not know of the racial history of the noose in the United States. (The student hailed from another nation.) I tend to agree that policing hate speech with specific sanctions for specific acts is a losing battle that does more harm than good. However, students were now asking a reasonable question: why did the university want to penalize protest and speech when students were speaking out against the president, but not when students were targeted?

I did not think that it was wise for Duke to charge these students with violating the community standard if they did nothing else that semester. I gave my view to the president and provost, and ultimately that was the policy the university adopted. My view was not based on a principled commitment to free speech, because I did not view the protest as an appropriate act of speech, it was really the suppression of the speech of others.

The Chair of the AC has no role in student judicial procedures, and I viewed myself as an intermediary between the students and the administration and was focused on trying to de-escalate tensions. There was hope—but no guarantee—that the peace could be kept through the end of the semester.

I attended a meeting before graduation during which a plan was devised to arrest any protesters who disrupted the graduation ceremony. A script was written, to be read at graduation, which would inform the assembled that disruptive protesters would be told that they were disrupting an event in an unauthorized manner, and that they would be arrested in thirty seconds if they did not stop. They would only receive one warning. The proposed order of ceremonies called for me, the chair of the faculty, to go to the microphone as arrests began and say, "Stay in your seats. Please remain calm. The ceremony will resume in five minutes." When a staff member read that phrase aloud in the Allen Building conference room, with the portraits of Duke president's past looking on, I burst out laughing. Stares ensued and I explained that the script reminded me of the scene in *Animal House* in which Kevin Bacon's character says, "Remain calm, all is well!" as the Founders Day parade spirals into John Belushi-fueled chaos. But I was the only one laughing. Things were tense.

I regrouped and shared my view that it would be a disaster if we arrested any of our students for protesting. I also told leaders of the protest group that it would be a huge error for their cause if they disrupted graduation, and they received similar advice from others. There were no protests on graduation weekend. And the students were not charged with honor code violations for their protest of President Price's Alumni Weekend speech. This seemed like a success at the time, however, looking back at this episode, I focused too much on trying to ensure that graduation was not marred by protest, and not enough about the role of protest as a part of the culture of dialogue and speech on a college campus. I had participated in papering over a vague policy that was not uniformly applied.

It turned out that there would be no shortage of things to protest at graduation in 2018. On May 2, a week before graduation, Vice President for Student Affairs Larry Moneta went to get a cup of tea and a muffin from the Joe Van Gogh coffee shop on Duke's campus. A rap song by the artist Young Dolph, with the refrain, "Get paid, young Nigga, get paid," was playing in the shop. Dr. Moneta objected to the lyrics and asked that the music be turned off, and it was. However, he also lodged a complaint with the owner of the establishment through the chain of command in his office, which was responsible for dining options on campus. The two baristas who were working that day were fired. This event became national news and President Price apologized for the actions of his vice president. Joe Van Gogh decided to close their campus shop due to the controversy.

Dr. Moneta was the university administrator whose office was responsible for adjudicating violations of the student code of conduct, including the protesters who interrupted the president a few weeks before, so he was involved in two crises simultaneously. To make matters worse, there were two instances of Racist speech in late April (the n word) being posted to social media by Duke students, and Dr. Moneta counseled the students to remove these posts and apologize, while pushing back against other students calling for the posters to be punished. Dr. Moneta responded to the request for punishment by posting also on social media that they should read Erwin Chemerinsky's book *Free Speech on Campus*, and he emphasized Chemerinsky's key point that attempts to regulate speech will inevitably be weaponized against vulnerable students and groups. What most angered students and faculty alike was his lecturing of students about having to bear objectionable speech targeted at them on principled grounds, while being unable to bear objectionable lyrics for the short time he was in a coffee shop. He then seemed to abuse his power by following up with the owner of the coffee shop.

My cell phone exploded when the coffee shop incident became public a few days after it occurred. Numerous faculty members were angry with Dr. Moneta due to the power dynamic on display over the coffee shop, and his past free speech absolutism that defended the right of people to use racial slurs. Both his inconsistency and his willingness to use the power of his position against people with less power had angered many faculty. He further asserted that it was his right as a customer to ask that the music be turned off. However, Dr. Moneta was not just any customer, but in charge of campus dining options, and his misuse of authority was particularly galling. Faculty who had tussled with Dr. Moneta over other issues during his twenty-year tenure at Duke were fed up, and some urged me to publicly call for Dr. Moneta's firing at the last Academic Council meeting of the 2017–18 academic year, days before graduation. This meeting threatened to spin out of control.

The Academic Council that I chaired became itself a target for the ire of some because we made no public statements, and a growing number of faculty members were writing me asking why we had "done nothing about the Moneta incident?" We had in fact been working feverishly behind the scenes since the incident became public on Tuesday, May 8, 2018, less than a week before the graduation ceremony.

The Academic Council (AC) and I had a new crisis to address at the time of the semester when everyone just wanted to finalize grades, celebrate a bit, and move into summer. The AC had a variety of views about the episode, as one would expect from a group of faculty elected from across the university. There was divergence over some of the particulars of what had transpired at Joe Van Gogh. We did have general agreement that once the music was turned off that the event should have been over, and what came next was Dr. Moneta wielding the power that he had in an unfair manner: a vice president versus a barista. Early on Thursday afternoon May 10, about ninety minutes before the AC meeting, I went to the Allen Building to meet with the president and Provost Sally Kornbluth. President Price was adamant that he did not think it appropriate to carry out personnel discussions in public as a matter of principle, and he noted the many years of service that Dr. Moneta had provided to Duke. They wanted to know if I was going to call for Dr. Moneta to resign or be fired at the AC meeting starting in an hour. I answered that I would not, because the executive committee had not reached consensus that this was the appropriate step for us to take. I then shared with the president and provost my personal perspective—Dr. Moneta should not be the vice president for student affairs in August 2018 when we welcomed a new class to campus. I suggested a sabbatical for him and then retirement, but that was not my decision.

Faculty colleagues had continued to email and text throughout the day, and two faculty members stopped me as I walked to the meeting asking why I had done nothing. I was feeling the pressure, and the meeting was tense. As the May 10 meeting began, I opened by reading the email that I had written to Vice President Moneta the day before. The main points that I raised on behalf of AC were that we felt he owed the baristas and the Duke community an apology for not letting the matter drop once the music was turned off, and then misusing his power by getting them fired. We emphasized the context of the event given recent discussions of racism on campus, discussions in which he had taken an absolutist stance on freedom of expression—except, apparently, when he was offended. I continued with my remarks and noted that Vice President Moneta felt that we were wrong and that he had acted appropriately. There was no miscommunication between us, we just viewed the situation differently. I noted that we offered Moneta an opportunity to address the council that day, but that he had declined.

President Price then spoke to the Council and answered questions. The AC meeting did not spin out of control, and the executive committee had managed to thread the needle and speak up directly to Dr. Moneta, letting the broader faculty know this, while operating behind the scenes with the president and provost. I made my personal views to them known, but what to do next was their decision as it should have been. Graduation weekend went off without a hitch and the Duke collective slumped into summer looking for rejuvenation. Dr. Moneta did retire after fifty years of service to higher education, and nearly twenty to Duke in May 2019—but not until after he sparked one last controversy that had racism and freedom of speech at its heart. And I was beginning to see a linkage between two issues that often seemed separate and whose champions did not seem to overlap. How could we at Duke encourage and expand dialogue and debate on campus, while protecting individuals asymmetrically affected by racist hate speech?

CHAPTER THREE: BROWNTOWN

To see what is in front of one's nose needs constant struggle

GEORGE ORWELL

A short conversation in May 2018 with my colleague Adrienne Lentz-Smith launched me on a journey of personal discovery that has transformed how I understand the impact of race and racism on my life. Adrienne and I were chatting about the modern South and recent events at Duke University, and I told her a story about my granddaddy losing a hunting dog near Browntown, a crossroads in Greene County, North Carolina. My Granddaddy Barrow's homeplace is where I spent summers harvesting tobacco as a kid, and the farm was between Arba and Jason, about four miles from Browntown.

Adrienne perked up and asked me why it was called Browntown. I replied, because that is where people of mixed race lived, and she followed up with, How and when did you learn that? I answered simply, a bit puzzled, that everyone knew that. This is a bad answer so far as historians are concerned, and she challenged me to look into the history of Browntown. I gave an afternoon to this effort in late May 2018 and visited the archives at the University of North Carolina at Chapel Hill. I found the process of archival research to be mesmerizing, and the sense of discovery when finding out how and when Browntown got its name captured my imagination and was the beginning of my genealogical research into my own family and reading North Carolina history.

As remarkable as the story itself was, I had never felt the need or desire to learn more about the history of Browntown or the people who lived there. My racial categorization of the people living there was all that I had needed to know, and this realization helped me to see that I would have to learn to first see racism in my own life, if I was going to play a part of addressing it on campus.

My casual categorization of everyone living in a place showed my lack of curiosity about a familiar place to me, but my research showed a long history of specific actions to create the idea underpinning Browntown: that some people are worth more than others. Piece by piece the story of Browntown's creation and maintenance came into focus through looking at primary sources like the digitized United States Census from 1790 to 1950, court cases resolving land disputes in the 1840s, newspaper accounts that referred to Browntown, and oral histories collected at various times through different means. I saw, by looking through last wills and testaments, how they documented the passage of wealth from one generation to the other in an around Browntown, with enslaved people being listed alongside land, mules, plow points and other bits of property. I discovered families that did not officially exist, created by the offspring of people who society said should not be making families together.

Around 1855, Benjamin S. Edwards, a wealthy farmer, purchased a 250-acre farm near Browntown Crossroads that remains a census place today. Benjamin Edwards purchased the farm for two of his children, Edith Edwards Hill and William Edwards, two years before he died. This was a banal transaction for a person of means in the 19th Century agrarian South, since this was how landed people passed on wealth to their offspring.

What is notable is that their mother, Eliza, was enslaved by their father, who received Eliza as a gift from his father Theophilus Edwards when she was only one year of age. Twelve years later they had their first child together. The gift of land served its purpose: both children lived on this farm at the 1900 Census, just as intended, along with their mother Eliza.

Benjamin Edwards, the enslaver who fathered Edith and William with Eliza, was one of the wealthiest men in Greene County as measured in the 1850 census. His homeplace and farm were in the north central part of Greene County, at a place called Tyson's Bridge, just north of Snow Hill, and it was valued at $20,000. His extended family owned several other large farms in this area, not very far from Browntown. This provides a sense of the connection of farmers to the land, and the soothing subtlety of repetitive seasonal farming, the year-after-year rhythm that provided a sense of stability as opposed to monotony. I drove past Browntown hundreds of times as a teen without a second thought. But now I understand Browntown to not only be a place, but most consequentially, an idea. Not White and not Black, but in between the poles of a clear hierarchy of value.

The daughter and son of Eliza, Edith, and William, born in 1830 and 1840 respectively, is straightforwardly mapped on ancestry.com, though nailing down with certainty the father of these two children is more difficult. It certainly seems to have been a member of the Edwards clan that owned Eliza, most likely Benjamin, who inherited "10 negroe slaves" from his father, Theophilus Edwards, in 1820. Among them was a child named Eliza, according to court documents. In 2014, Eliza's 106-year-old great granddaughter, Arlena Hill LaBon, described her origin story in a March 4, 2014, article for the *Kinston (NC) Free Press* as beginning when her great-grandfather a "White Englishman," brought her great-grandmother, a slave, from England to settle in North Carolina. Arlena omitted names and instead focused on the fact that one of her great grandparents owned the other.

Arlena's father, Silas P. "Jack" Hill, was one of the

grandchildren that Benjamin Edwards would never meet. He lived with his wife, Patsy Sugg Hill, and their children and farmed the Browntown land that Benjamin provided for his children and their descendants. One February morning in 1923, eight years after the death of Jack's mother—Edith, the child of an enslaved woman and an enslaver herself—Jack and his daughter Arlena went to the store in Snow Hill owned by Josiah Caull Exum, Sr. and found themselves in a one-sided negotiation—an offer that Jack couldn't refuse. Jack Hill came seeking to buy provisions on credit from the prominent store owner to tide the family farm over until the fall harvest, an annual ritual even for those with land but who were not wealthy, regardless of race. He left with flour, sugar, coffee, rice, and tears in his eyes.

According to Arlena's account, Josiah Exum provided the dry goods but told Jack Hill, "You don't have to pay me back the $500, I will just take your farm once your wife Patsy dies." Arlena, who died at 108 years of age in 2016, said that her father had to comply, since a "colored man" had been "hung on a tree" at the Greene County courthouse for "talking back." The fear of being lynched rendered Jack Hill unable to push back against the offer that his daughter recounted. Jack Hill left the farm twenty-one years later upon the death of his wife and moved to a house on Harper Street in Snow Hill, where he died in 1949 more than two decades after he was initially threatened with murder if he did not agree to the plan foisted upon him and completed much later.

Arlena Hill LaBon told a story of slow-motion land theft, a one-sided deal borne of coercion under the threat of lynching that was used to circumvent the most basic function of government —the protection of private property. Equal protection under the law was supposed to be the standard, but it did not apply equally to people living in Browntown in the 1920 and 1930s. The descendants of a prominent rich enslaver and the woman he enslaved were no match in a land dispute with a prominent White merchant, in spite of the fact that by 1923 the descendants of Benjamin and Eliza Edwards had owned their Browntown farm for about half the time since the ratification of the United States Constitution, and more than fifty years after the ratification of the Thirteenth and Fourteenth Amendments that codified equal protection under the law for all people. The protection that Browntown afforded the family for more than half a century, had eroded by the 1920s when not being White meant not having power. They lost their farm because they needed credit during a time when Jim Crow laws and the political climate of the day made the Thirteenth through the Fifteenth amendments to the Constitution little more than words on a piece of paper.

There are several aspects of Arlena Hill Labon's story, recorded over eighty years after the fact, that I could not confirm in my research, but its essence holds up. Numerous archival records, including census documents and a last will and testament, show that Eliza was born into slavery in North Carolina to her mother Nance (no last name given), and not only was Benjamin born in North Carolina, but so were both of his parents and all his siblings. Numerous archival records and public family trees on ancestry.com document Eliza giving birth to Edith Edwards Hill and her brother William Edwards, just as Arlena LaBon said, though I have not found stronger proof, such as a family Bible, that Benjamin S. Edwards was their father. I have confirmed the general story with another descendant of Eliza Edwards whom I met via ancestry.com, who knew the name of the father of Eliza's children only as "Slave Master Edwards." I told her of my reasoning as to why I believed Benjamin to be the patriarch of the family, but she had no information to confirm or deny this supposition or provide other information.

The essence of Arlena's story—that her father feared disagreeing with a prominent White store owner because of threats of violence—rings true, due to a highly publicized 1916 lynching in Greene County, a story that would have been widely known and repeated still in 1923. Joseph Black, the father of sixteen-year-old Will Black, was lynched in Greene County (spirited away from the Lenoir County courthouse in Kinston, about fifteen miles away, but taken back to Greene County to be murdered) after he was jailed when he sought to help his son defend himself against charges that the teen had sexually assaulted a six year-old White girl and her mother. The nearby *Wilson Daily News* began a July 7, 1916, story describing the court inquiry into the April 5, 1916, lynching in this way.

"The great hand of the law yesterday reached down into the tree of iniquity, shook it, and there fluttered down and fell many possibilities, a mist of depression that enshrouded two counties and ripe fruit of realization that the commonwealth is intent upon avenging its fair name blotted with the blood of Joe Black upon whom a mob inflicted death because he had dared to threaten a White man and to assert that his flesh and blood was equal to his."

The story went on to note the names of fourteen men who were that day implicated in open court of the lynching by the testimony of a detective, H.B. Barnes:

"These men include some of the most prominent citizens of Greene County. The kinspeople of some of them can be found in nearly every neighborhood of all the counties around."

One of the citizens who participated in the lynching was a justice of the peace and a prominent farmer, Samuel Stocks, was indicted for his participation. This didn't stop sixteen-year-old Will Black from being executed in the electric chair on July 21, 1916, a month after he was convicted in a trial that lasted twenty-three minutes—including the time the jury deliberated. Josiah Caull Exum, the storekeeper who Arlena said took her daddy's farm, was not implicated in the 1916 lynching. It was simply a well-known episode that would have made threats of violence whether explicit or implied seem very real.

As I dug, the story got more complicated. On January 18, 1935, Josie D. Exum, the wife of Josiah Caull Exum, purchased 108 acres of land sold at auction because of unpaid property taxes, on the front steps of the Greene County courthouse. Jack Hill and family continued to live on the farm until his wife died, just as

Josiah Exum promised when he threatened Jack. Did Jack Hill stop paying taxes after being threatened with lynching by Josiah Exum during the 1923 encounter at his store, assuming that the farm would no longer be his anyway? It is unclear. However, there is a bill of sale for the land, though the chain of events that lead to the sale began with a threat of murder. There was a modicum of legal cover for the sale of the farm that was nevertheless coerced. The most valuable aspect of a tobacco farm in Greene County in 1935 was the ability to buy and sell tobacco as defined in the price support program that was instituted by the federal government in 1933 to help pull the nation out of the depression.

The Hill family lived on this farm for decades after the Civil War, paying their bills from their farming and never resorting to mortgaging the farm according to Census records reviewed from 1870 to 1930. This lack of mortgage debt does not make sense alongside a family losing a farm because they could not pay property taxes—surely a person would mortgage a property before losing it to foreclosure. This circumstantial evidence and the fact that Jack Hill lived on the farm until his wife died just as the earlier account noted, suggests the threat of violence is what lead to the sale of the farm.

No record can be found dividing the original 250-acre farm that was purchased by Benjamin Edwards to care for his children divided into separate parcels—one for the son and the other for the daughter. This would have been a common practice, but without proof of such a division, the sale of the 108 acres that Mrs. Exum bought on the courthouse steps in 1935 would not be legal even if the sale had not been coerced. In 1972, an heir of Josiah Exum unsuccessfully sought to enforce a 'quit claim' deed on the disputed portion of the original farm, and Calvin Edwards, a descendant of William Edwards, and the great great-great-grandson of Benjamin and Eliza Edwards, owned the adjacent farm that was surveyed in the 1980s as being 126 acres in size.

The Greene County courthouse burned in 1876, taking with it any primary records of the original sale of the land in the

1850s, or whether the farm was divided into separate parcels for the children of Benjamin and Eliza Edwards. Such a division of land was a common occurrence in the nineteenth century as well as today in the rural South, but the destruction of records in the courthouse fire makes numerous details impossible to untangle. Key elements of this story will likely never be resolved, but any dispute over land ownership between a prominent White merchant and a Browntown farmer in the 1920s and 1930s was always going to be decided in Josiah Exum's favor, since he was White and Jack Hill was not—the threat of racially motivated violence would have been real.

Changing Meaning of Browntown

The relative social status of Browntown changed across time, as what it meant to be of mixed race changed. There seems to have been a protective effect for much of the last third of the nineteenth century, as Browntown residents were viewed as being closer to White than Black, because it was wealthy White men who had seen to the creation of this place. While the story of wealthy White enslaver impregnating a Black enslaved woman, he owned is a common story of the antebellum South, providing the subsequent family with a 250-acre Tobacco farm was not the most common response to such a union. Edith and William were both enslaved people upon their birth, and there is no record of Benjamin Edwards issuing a bill of manumission—the practice of giving freedom to enslaved people upon the death of their owner. Because the slave schedules of the 1850 and 1860 Census enumerations do not contain the names of the enslaved, it is impossible to definitively track where Eliza and her two children were living in those years. William Edwards was 20 in 1850 and could have been working on the farm as an enslaved person, or working as an overseer of other enslaved people, or something in between. It would have taken substantial labor to tend a 250-acre farm.

Edith and William Edwards and their Mother Eliza, a family created from the unequal power inherent with chattel slavery seems to have lived in relative peace for nearly half a century, through the Civil War, Reconstruction, the push back against Reconstruction, and the move into the twentieth century and the rollback of voting rights for Blacks in North Carolina. Browntown was closer to White than Black before and after the Civil War and being in the lineage of one of the wealthiest White men in Greene County must have helped the family's fortunes, even after Benjamin died in 1857.

Newspaper stories commonly referred to Browntown as a "mixed-race" community from the 1850s until the late nineteenth century. However, it was described as a Negro community during the first two decades of the twentieth century. For example, I found news stories in the nearby *Kinston Free Press* and the *Standard Laconic* in 1921 about a bear being loose in the area, and the pieces noted that Browntown was a Negro community, a simple fact in a story that had nothing to do with race. Any privilege and protection that emanated from the offspring of wealthy landowners living in the area in the 1850s was gone seventy years later. This demonstrates the changing relative social status of Browntown that affected the descendants of Benjamin and Eliza Edwards. By the 1920s and 1930s, Browntown had lost any relative protection that may have been conferred because the patriarch was a wealthy White man, and the bedrock American value of equal protection under the law did not apply. Jack Hill's farm was taken from him because he was not White.

The phrase *social construction of race* is common parlance in the social sciences and humanities and is likely heard as academic bullshit by many outside of the academy. It is nothing of the sort, but the real-life way in which people with power use race to keep theirs and get more. The idea of Browntown demonstrates this at work. Rich, powerful White enslavers decided that they wanted to provide a modicum of protection to the families they saw fit to create with enslaved women, and a point of protection between Black and White was created. Their power and prestige are what made this work. Decades later, the memory of wealthy plantation owners was no longer as relevant, and the context of Jim Crow meant that not being White made you vulnerable, and especially if you owned an asset like a prime tobacco farm. The U.S. census files for Greene County from 1850 to 1920 provide an example. Edith Edwards Hill was born in 1830, and her location cannot be mapped with certainty in 1840 because only the head of household is listed by name. The 1850 and 1860 census counts include so-called Slave schedules that named only the owner and provided sex and age of those who were enslaved. In the 1870 Census, Edith Hill is listed as having race of Mulatto, but in 1880 she is listed as Black. The 1890 Census burned and is lost. Edith's race is recorded at the last three Census counts before her death in 1927 (1900-1920) as Black, Mulatto and Black. The changing race in the Census did not represent variations in how they self-identified during this time range, but what the census official "saw" when they took the count and what they knew, thought and assumed. Race being assigned to an individual by someone in this way is the social construction of race in action. And whatever protective effect Browntown may have provided in the past was gone when Jack Hill had his farm taken according to his daughter's account many years later. It is worth underlining that in 1923, the farm had been in Jack Hill's family for half of the time the United States had been a country.

The census enumerations from 1790 through 1950 have been digitized and are publicly available in a format that is easy to read and use for research. The census provides two choices —a digitized version and a picture of the original handwritten entries. Some of the entries are beautifully written and some are illegible because actual people went to do the counting. There are numerous transcription errors so the work can be tedious. However, seeing the handwriting of the 1900 Greene County census taker, James Smith, writing the name Eliza Edwards, made dusty history alive to me and it gave me a sense of the triumph and progress that we have made in the United States. She was being counted as a full person even though she was born an enslaved person. As I was documenting her multi-generational household, I glanced at some of the other entries on the same census page, since my people are also from the same part of Greene County. The Census entries are laid out in the order of when the enumerator visited a home to undertake the count. When Mr. Smith left the Edwards home on June 14, 1900, he went next to the tobacco farm owned by a White man named Henry Lee Sugg, who lived there with his wife and five children. They were tobacco farmers just like the Edwards clan and every other family within miles. As I looked at the flowing handwriting, I let out an audible gasp and my wife asked, "What's wrong?" I answered simply, "My Great-Grandmother Blanche Sugg lived in the adjacent farm to Eliza Edwards and her children at the 1900 Census." A casual interest turned into an obsession.

CHAPTER FOUR: RECKONING WITH MYSELF

Don't focus on the speck in your brother's eye, focus on the log in your own

JESUS, (MATTHEW 7:3)

Learning the history of Browntown got my attention as did my great grandmother living next door to a woman born into slavery. This connection made history feel alive and not ancient because my Grandmother Maxine had talked to me about her mother Blanche. I loved someone who loved her. I continue to learn more about my family legacy and have connected with a public history group that is run by current and former residents of Browntown who want to tell the story of the people living there on their own terms.

Learning more about this history helped me begin to understand that the many casual judgments I made about race as an adolescent, and continuing as an adult, led me to see some people as worth more than others. Such judgments could be triggered by nothing more than a glance at skin color. If you asked me if that was the case directly, I would have said, 'of course not, each human being is created equally in the eyes of God and the Constitution.' However, my subconscious reality was different, and this affected me because it influenced how I interacted with others.

A memory that illustrates what I mean is from the day my parents moved me into my college dormitory in August 1986. There was a mixed-race couple helping students to move their belongings into the dorm—the man was White, and the woman was Black. They were obviously a couple given their displays of affection for one another, and the novelty and the openness of this relationship led me to look twice on several occasions. I had to keep reminding myself not to stare. However, it was more than that. It was the racial makeup of the coupling. As I have unpacked this memory in writing this book and thought about why this is one of the primary things I remember from that day, two reasons come to mind. First, this couple was notable because of how open and comfortable they were in public with one another. I simply had not seen that growing up in rural eastern North Carolina. Mixed-race couples signified scandal or were at minimum unusual and against the normal order of things. Second, my assumption was that Black men desired White women and not vice versa. This is really what had me turning my head to stare.

What I have since learned about Browntown demonstrated that my assumption about mixed-race couples was ahistorical. The original idea of Browntown was to create a place to live for the families that wealthy White enslavers created with women they enslaved. It was a place between White and Black, and these children were born into slavery and remained the property of their father unless they received papers of manumission from him. The idea of Browntown lived on into my adolescence; I'd often heard a "joke" between older and younger White boys about going to Browntown to "get some experience with girls." That was a continuation of the idea that some people remained available for White men if we so desired. Race served as the marker of value. When I blithely explained to my historian colleague that

Browntown was a place where mixed-race people lived, I did so without knowing or thinking about the history that created a place that I knew was defined by race.

It was well into my time as a professor at Duke that I no longer commonly had an urge to look twice when seeing a Black and White couple strolling hand in hand around Duke University's campus. These were powerful, subconscious responses that were triggered by a glance, and had nothing to do with the people strolling by. Ideas are powerful and persistent, more so than monuments of stone. With practice, I controlled this unthinking tic by addressing it head on with an internal dialogue. Why do you care about who someone else loves? They are free to choose their own partners. Don't look twice. Old habits and ideas can be thwarted, but only if you name them as a problem, and replace them with something else, another idea. I had to undertake a conscious effort to replace an assumption that mixed-race couples were scandalous or notable. This was a personal problem that I learned to address based on what I understood to be right. However, I did not delve into how these ideas were formed in my head, heart, and soul over the course of my life. That is, until the season of reflection during my time as chair of the AC at Duke.

Lessons from My Family Legacy

My Granddaddy P.L. Barrow was a central figure of my life until his death in 1987. After his death, I began piecing together information about his life with my Grandmother Maxine, as part of my genealogical research. He was a tobacco farmer who did not graduate from high school but went on to be a member of the local school board and later served as sheriff of Greene County from 1963 to 1978. Over the summer of 2018, I spent a lot of time investigating my granddaddy's life, seeking to fill in blanks and to amplify things that I knew only generally. For example, during the summer of 1967 just before I was born, he hired two Black deputy sheriffs. On July 14, 1967, *The Standard Laconic* newspaper reported this event, and he was quoted as saying:

"With the large number of Negro nights to be patrolled in order to keep law and order there was a definite need for temporary help. This was the reason for the hiring of James Hines and Claude Smith."

The help was not temporary and Deputy Hines, who happened to be from Browntown, was someone that I got to know in the mid-to-late 1970s because he remained a deputy sheriff until he retired. This quotation is certainly not a rousing call to equality in the language of civil rights, but instead a practical answer from a stoic man to a straightforward question. He would commonly answer questions with "yes" or "no" replies. We only discussed this decision once, during the summer of 1987 after my freshman year at the University of North Carolina at Chapel Hill, just a few weeks before he died. I had learned about the civil rights movement during my freshman year in college, and I had a question. "Why did you hire two Black deputies?"

"About half the folks in Greene County are Black, so it made sense to have Black deputies" he replied.

I pushed a bit, and he offered only a little more. "The hardest part of being a sheriff" he said, "was serving warrants and summons to people's houses. When a White deputy went to a Black family's house, it made things more tense." The language of civil rights to which I had been exposed during my freshman year in college was not part of his explanation to me. He was simply saying that the local sheriff's department did not match what the community of people who lived where he served, needed. My learning continues and I recently met the grandson of one of the first two Black deputies, who is also interested in genealogy and the idea of a "tri-identity" of Black, White and Native American given the legacy of Tuscarora Indians in Greene County. There is an emerging culture of public history telling a history that was not taught in school, at least to me.

My summers living with my Grandparents Barrow, when I

worked on their tobacco farm as an adolescent and teen, were fundamental in my formation as a person and I am grateful for our time together. I regret that my interest in family legacy only began after both died, robbing me of the opportunity to ask questions about how race governed things across the course of their lives. I had plenty of opportunities to be more curious about these matters of course, especially with my grandmother who did not die until 2016, but my interest was not piqued until they both were gone.

Glimpsing White as Identity

The concept of identity is central to many issues on a college campus, and the central question at hand is often about who gets to define reality. My summary description of Browntown labeled others, but I did not think of myself as having an identity at all. I was just myself and viewed being White as simply a fact. Doing archival research has helped me to better understand the process of how one's identity can be imposed upon them. Learning this history that had been right under my nose all my life caused me to think and wonder: have I ever experienced White as an identity that was imposed upon me by others, and not simply a fact?

I spent the summer of 1989 in Pakistan completing an internship for my undergraduate degree in Public Health. That summer gave me the new experience of standing out simply because I looked different from those around me. Even when people were friendly and hospitable, as they typically were, I experienced the second and third glances as stressful. I was used to blending in and going about my business without anyone noticing, but that was impossible for me in Pakistan. My identity as a White American could have exposed me to danger one day —not because of who I was as an individual, but because of what others might assume about me from a casual glance. The identity that they could impose upon me given the situation.

The day after the leader of Iran, Ayatollah Ruhollah

Khomeini, died at age 89, I was in Rawalpindi, walking past the confluence of main roads near the Raja bazaar, the city's hub of commerce. I was not only White and a head taller than many in the crowd, but my presence screamed American—I was wearing an Indiana Jones-style fedora. That identity had not posed any problems for me so far that summer, but as I walked through the bazaar, shouting and wailing drew my attention to a small group that was flagellating themselves with whips—repetitively striking their own backs in what I believed to have been a Shi'a Muslim mourning ritual. Shias are a minority within Pakistan, but the Ayatollah was a key leader in the Islamic world, Iran shares a border with Pakistan, and Pakistani Prime Minister Benazir Bhutto had declared a period of national mourning upon the report of the imam's death. A nearby shopkeeper got my attention as I stared at the commotion, and said "you need to get off the street for a while, come and take tea."

I went with him through his shop to a back room and sat and sipped milky sweet tea as he told me briefly that the Ayatollah had died. He suggested I stay put in his shop until things calmed down a bit, and I did so. A short time later, I thanked the man and went on my way after the commotion had passed. I had been shown kindness by a stranger who had looked out for me, and I wasn't harmed or even threatened. On that day in 1989 in a crowded bazaar in Pakistan, I stood out due to my identity as a White American, based solely on my appearance, and the color of my skin. My summer in Pakistan provided me with an experience of the race-induced stress of standing out, but I did not have the insight at twenty-one to bring this lesson home with me in a way that transformed my understanding of how race operated in my own country. Instead, I settled back into my assumption of White as a fact and this memory was simply one of many from a summer of discovery.

My education, both formal and taught through family lore, was incomplete at best, and the past few years reading North Carolina and United States history have proven to be eye opening. The first governor impeached and removed from office in the United States was William Holden, so removed in 1871 for putting down a Ku Klux Klan rebellion in Alamance County. Holden occupied the county with state troops to protect freed slaves and allied Whites who were trying to move on from the Civil War to forge a new nation, but they were being murdered and their homes burned. And for this, Governor Holden was removed from office. The only *coup d'état* in U.S. history took place in the familiar eastern North Carolina port city of Wilmington in 1898, where I often played football and golf, but I did not learn of this in school. Charles B. Aycock, the most famous person from my hometown of Goldsboro, North Carolina, was indeed "the education governor" as we were taught during visits to his homeplace—but he was also the architect of a plan to make it much harder for Blacks to vote, while making it easier for Whites via a change in the state constitution.

We need more and better history, not less. The second Trump administration has moved rapidly in 2025 to rid government agencies, universities and businesses of DEI, even as the term remains undefined. Some states got a head start on such efforts, like Florida, where universities and the public schools are not allowed to teach certain facts and ideas that might upset White students. This trend is escalating, nationally. My alma mater UNC recently banned jobs in the state university system that focus on DEI or any adjacent ideas. I would gladly trade all DEI programming for a faithful wrestling with U.S. history, especially since the end of the Civil War. We should wrestle with how this history affects us today, and we may not all agree, but that is the point. We need to learn to talk with one another and listen.

The family lore that was passed on was similarly incomplete. The television miniseries *Roots* that premiered when I was ten years old in 1977, was the first time I recall thinking about the legacy of slavery in the United States. I recall banter at family reunions and similar gatherings where a basic claim was sometimes made. "We fought in the Revolutionary War, and the Civil War, but we did not own any slaves," went the arc of the story. The story turned out to be false for at least part of my family. Online genealogical research shows that both my Great-Great-Grandfather Joseph Sugg (1830–1916) and his father Lemuel Sugg (1808–1870) each owned slaves as recorded in the 1850 and 1860 slave schedules. Both ancestors are buried in the Sugg family graveyard that is behind the still-standing house that my Great-Grandmother Blanche lived in at the 1900 Census, on the farm adjacent to the freed slave Eliza Edwards. It was Eliza's grandson whose farm was taken in the episode described in Chapter Three of this book. Note that I do not think that it is surprising that landed farmers in Greene County, N.C. owned Slaves in the 19th Century. What is most interesting to me is my seeing this documented in the 1850 and 1860 Slave Schedules was a discovery. Interestingly enough, when I first began my genealogical research with Ancestry, I did so with the default settings at the time, which excluded searches of the Slave schedules. A librarian showed me how to expand my search.

The more I learned, the closer this history felt to my life.

So many of the discoveries that I have made about the role of race in my life were right under my nose all the time. My parents moved out of the house where I grew up and into a continuing care retirement community in March 2019 and I drove home to Goldsboro in late February to clean out my bedroom to prepare for the house to be sold, and for them to move. I took my time looking through all the memorabilia and artifacts of the 1970s and 1980s that were in my old bedroom, and I was mesmerized by the contents of boxes, folders, and drawers: looking, feeling, touching, reading, and remembering. Old newspaper clippings, notes scribbled to and from old girlfriends, ticket stubs from the high school prom, a program from the 1981 Sugar Bowl, and so on. One long forgotten item that caught my eye was a cigar box wedged under a shoe tree in the back of my closet that contained a collection of arrowheads. These trinkets, untouched for three or four decades, nudged me back to my summers spent living in Greene County with my grandparents, harvesting tobacco from age ten until college. I remembered that arrowheads were plentiful in the fields, especially when a moldboard plow was used to prepare land for the growing season each February, bringing to the surface what was buried and submerging what was on top to start a new growing season. This rhythm of the fields had persisted for centuries in eastern North Carolina.

Sometimes I picked up arrowheads found in the fields as a boy and put them in my pocket, while other times I would just step over them, or skip them across my Granddaddy's mill pond. And some had been saved in my closet and forgotten, not seen since the mid-1980s. As I sat on the floor and rubbed the arrowheads, I realized that it never crossed my mind when finding arrowheads as a boy to ask the simple question, "Where did all the American Indians go?"

That is what I would have asked if I had managed to be curious about common things that surrounded me when I was young. Browntown was not the only thing that was under my nose that I managed to ignore growing up. The history of where I grew up had always been more complex than only Black and White. The new reality (to me) at Duke was that both the Black/White issues, as well as anti-Asian racism, anti-Semitism, and other forms of prejudice on campus, were linked. They were all forms of the idea that some are worth more than others. There were layers and layers of history, just like in the Greene County soil, and I just needed to pay attention and be willing to learn.

Later that semester a faculty colleague at UNC suggested that I should read David La Vere's excellent book, *The Tuscarora War*, when she heard me talking about Greene County. The massacre and displacement of American Indians during the early years of the 18th century, and the selling of some into slavery, stunned me. Not because I did not understand that American Indians have been displaced, massacred, and enslaved during the last 300 years, but because it took place in Greene County, providing me with new context to understand why arrowheads were plentiful on my granddaddy's farm. The transition of my parents to a retirement community was just another opportunity to better understand my past, therefore helping me to be a better leader moving forward at Duke. And a more empathetic human being.

My entire life has been racialized even though I rarely thought about race until I was age 30. This means race was the most persistent force that determined what people did around me, how they acted and where they could go daily. This was true when growing up in Eastern, North Carolina and remais true today. A key reality is that it was possible for me to live most of my life without thinking much about the realities of race and how they affected me—because I am a White man. It was easy for me to not have to think about it, and it has become clear to me that this is not the case for everyone. My life experience has not included being held out of places or opportunities due to my race. I am not telling you that you have not—this is my story. The persistence of race as an influence in my life was a new insight for me, and it focused my attention on Black versus White, which had been my experience growing up, as well as my family's multi-generational experience in agrarian eastern North Carolina. However, at a global university like Duke, it was not all Black and White. I still struggle at times to break out of the Black/White dichotomy. I remain a work in progress as we all are.

CHAPTER FIVE: FREE EXPRESSION V. PROTECTION IN A GLOBAL UNIVERSITY

Between the wish and the thing, the world lies waiting

CORMAC MCCARTHY, ALL THE PRETTY HORSES

Two days before fall classes started at Duke in 2018, someone scribbled the word *nigger* on a sign for the Mary Lou Williams Center for Black Culture. The class of 2022 experienced racism-driven campus turmoil before attending a class at the university. President Price wrote in an email to the Duke community as students finalized their course schedules:

"Someone scrawled a heinous racial epithet . . . Such a cowardly and hateful act has absolutely no place in our community. While we can't undo or unsee this painful assault on our right to live and study in a civil and respectful environment, we can and do promise that odious acts like this will be acknowledged and challenged at every opportunity, especially at a time when some seek to deliberately sow hatred and distrust."

President Price had hoped to reset the campus discussion on racism to a scholarly consideration of Duke's history, primed by his decision to leave empty the space that had held the Lee statue in front of the Duke Chapel for the foreseeable future, and his instruction to identify a campus location to serve as a hub for this research and learning. His plan was a good one that was nevertheless overtaken by events. My second year as chair of the AC was marked by a series of high-profile racist incidents on campus that targeted different groups, making clear the global nature of the bigotry on campus that could disrupt the intellectual culture of debate. We bounced from crisis to crisis and did not manage to focus our efforts to address racism as lead by faculty with expertise in relevant fields.

In September, a mural painted on the East Campus free speech bridge by the group *Mi Gente* in honor of Latina Heritage month was defaced. A swastika was carved into a bathroom stall on campus in October. Antisemitic fliers were left around campus in November. Each incident had unique facts but also a familiar rhythm. Could words and symbols of any kind be painted on the free expression bridge between East and West Campuses? Was anonymous speech the same as owning one's words? Was defacing speech itself a kind of speech? Were the perpetrators students, or outsiders whose goal was to embroil the campus for their own purposes? The swastika is a unique global, cross-cultural symbol of annihilation and genocide of Jews, and if anti-Semitism was growing on and around campus, this portended other forms of extremism taking root and thriving.

When incidents occurred and the university expressed outrage and support, other groups clamored for acknowledgment of their unique pain both present and past. Or students brought up horrific examples of mistreatment that were not acknowledged at Duke, such as the persecution of the Uighurs in China, or the treatment of Armenians in Nagorno-Karabakh. There was a sense of a zero-sum amount of empathy and outrage available in the community, with disparate groups making claims for it. And there is a limit to how much attention and energy a university can and should put toward a particular incident. After all, the purpose of the university is research and teaching. It is difficult to strike the correct balance between speaking out, when to do so, and what to say in response to racist incidents on campus. Universities run the risk of elevating the voices of those making anonymous slurs by denouncing all such incidents. And then, a university must figure out how to put local events into a global context and vice versa. This remains work in progress at Duke and in all universities today.

One of my biggest regrets as chair of the AC was not understanding and expressing that the problems we were seeing in reduced debate and free expression on campus and the need to protect members targeted by racist speech were two sides of the same coin. They are commonly seen as being in tension, and there are fixes to the second problem that could make the first worse. However, clarity that racist speech has an asymmetric impact on some individuals and groups is a fact that should be acknowledged, even if we are uncertain that we can devise a cure that is not worse than the disease.

If I could travel through time back to the start of the new academic year 2018 I would tell myself and anyone who would listen three things. First, racism of all types inflames the intellectual community of the campus more so than other issues, because at bigotry's heart lays the idea that some are worth more than others. Universities are supposed to proceed by judging evidence using the standards of the disciplines, and symbols like the swastika and noose represent the opposite. Second, the intellectual community at Duke needs to work to assimilate our student body into a social-media aware community, that values reasoned debate and provides protection to targeted members by saying clearly that they belong—they are one of us, and we are a part of them because we share a campus. Third, faculty experts in controversial topics should lead as we seek to create on campus what we take for granted in our research—communities that share evidentiary standards that govern how we fight things out intellectually. The goal of faculty should be to help students develop the shared norms that will lead to robust debate, discussion and consideration of how, when and why people should change their mind. This is more about process than it is a position on any given topic.

There was an understandable desire of university leadership to ride out each crisis and remain focused on research and teaching. However, what we were also doing was allowing the campus intellectual community to atrophy, and we were not providing students with enough opportunity to practice making the case while listening to others doing the same. There were many faculty with research expertise in race and related areas, as well as those who are experts on First Amendment law and dialogue, but they were not typically a part of university responses that seemed designed to survive the crisis at hand instead of risking "breaking back into jail" and addressing the root problems. I regret not understanding the opportunity we had to simply practice talking more openly about racist attacks in our community, informed by the scholarship of faculty with research expertise in related topics, as intellectual growth opportunities. Naming targeted students as full members of the community and more openly discussing Duke and Durham's shared history of which race is central could have helped our students develop resilience against such attacks, so that they were not repetitively derailed from their studies, work and social lives.

Because we did not correctly frame the racist-incident-driven turmoil on campus as an intellectual issue, it was most commonly viewed through the lens of community standard violations, which rightly focused on intent in judging any violation, as opposed to the impact on campus expression and debate. Similarly, anonymous slurs touched off unproductive discussions of whether perpetrators were outsiders or members of the community, which of course is necessary if the mode of response is primarily adjudicating potential community standard violations. We missed an opportunity to talk more clearly about the reality that hate speech has an asymmetric impact on different members of a community—it is an attempt to hold out groups from membership in the intellectual community who were historically prevented from joining. Naming and talking about the tension between expression and protection is a process that could have expanded speech while demonstrating that targeted community members were valued and full members. This would be shown by the community standing up for them and saying that they belong and not focusing on punishment for perpetrators. I failed to understand this as chair of the AC at the time, and that was a consequential error.

Navigating the line between free expression and protection is an old issue for the academy as well as for Duke. The university's first public crisis around the free speech v protection debate was the 1903 Bassett Affair, when Duke university was still Trinity College and located on the current East Campus land. John Bassett was a professor of history who wrote a book that asserted that Booker T. Washington was "all in all the greatest man, save General Lee, born in the South in 100 years." He compared and extolled their shared merit to the outrage of the conservative political party of that day in North Carolina, the Democrats. What was controversial 120 years ago was comparing a Black man, regardless of how great, to Robert E. Lee, the symbol of the defeated Confederacy. Ironically, the removal of Lee from the front of the Duke Chapel in 2017 demonstrated that while the positions of the political parties had switched, and what was viewed as controversial had changed, the debate was essentially the same. Where was the line around what could be said on campus? And who decided? The Trinity Board of Trustees decided not to accept Professor Bassett's resignation by a vote of 18 to 7, and instead made a statement supporting academic freedom and the ability of scholars to speak in the language of their academic discipline as they wished and could defend. This incident is rightly celebrated as a victory of academic freedom, yet one that was won in something quite less than unanimous fashion. That tension is a part of this foundational story of Duke that is often papered over.

Speech Codes Are a Medicine Worse Than the Disease

A Duke University Commission on Hate and Bias that was created by the former president and provost in 2015 reported out to the community in April 2016 with a warning about the difficult equipoise between freedom of expression, academic freedom and freedom of speech and protection:

"**Clarifying Bias and Hate Incidents**. Based on our review of practices at Duke and at other institutions, it is clear that articulating a definition of bias and hate has been challenging. Government organizations have established some definitions, but the issues are especially complex in a campus environment charged with balancing the free exchange of ideas and the safety and well-being of the community." (see P. 23. Brownell and Burton 2016).

This passage is true enough—it is especially complex in a campus environment that must balance free exchange and safety in a pluralistic and diverse community, but the report did not focus on the idea that more and better speech could crowd out the bad. They had rightly discussed both the difficulty of parsing speech to determine what was objectionable and a violation of our community standard, and the danger of unintended consequences of seeking to do so. However, the work stopped there and what was needed was a call to work on the nature of the intellectual community that we now had at Duke, and to openly state that we were going to move toward difficulty and err on the side of more speech, while seeking to better understand the protections that may be needed on campus. We needed to normalize talking about these paradoxes, and to allow our students opportunities to practice doing so. We need to be clearer about wanting more and better speech and that increased protection for more vulnerable members of the community best comes via more speech, not less.

The 2015 commission was formed to address the fallout of a noose being hung on a campus tree by an undergraduate student near the Black student cultural center. The image of the noose was widely circulated on social media leading to fear on campus because it was unclear who had placed the symbol in the heart of campus near the student center. Even folks posting it in outrage —"Oh my God, I cannot believe this, it is terrible" helped to spread its impact. Students wondered, Was the perpetrator a fellow hallmate in my dorm? The person next to me on the campus bus? Or my class lab partner? The student came forth and confessed while insisting that they did not understand the meaning of the noose as a symbol of anti-Black racism in the American South because they were an undergraduate student who graduated from high school in another nation. This explanation was met with skepticism around the campus but also underlined the international nature of the undergraduate student body. We rightly celebrated the diversity of our students but often did so in congratulatory fashion that did not consider how undergraduates were to be assimilated into the culture of expression and debate at Duke. The hope was that the commission could provide a way forward, but there was no agreement on balancing the need for better education about racism and bias, with legislating words and symbols that could not be said on campus. The broader faculty were not part of this discussion, which was a mistake because the ability of the disciplines to discuss, disagree and debate was the essence of what we needed *writ large* at Duke. This was a classic example of a commission in many ways freezing discussion and slowing opportunities to move forward.

A stalemate developed and we were stuck as a community. Racist incidents that garnered much attention kept happening each month or so, and we could not reach consensus as a campus on what to do about it. We both overreacted and underreacted. We overreacted by being at the mercy of a racist event and either being compelled as a university to issue a statement or having to justify why we did not. We underreacted by not better amplifying the work of scholars who had long been studying these issues to help us better understand racism on campus and beyond. We seemed to forget that we had numerous scholars who could have led us from their position of academic expertise. University officers fear elevating the voices of faculty on such issues because they cannot be controlled due to academic freedom. However, the only comparative advantage the university has as an organization *is* the faculty, and at Duke there are world renowned scholars of race, and the impact of race on politics, health, and education and so on. They should have been elevated as leaders of how to address these problems. That remains the case today.

Efforts to get ahead of these incidents could not find footing. All the oxygen was sucked out of the room by our having to navigate the serial incidents, while campus members parsed statements issued by the president's office or fumed that he had not issued a statement after another incident, on campus or off. It was particularly difficult to navigate the specific facts of each incident, which was the focus of the university, especially with respect to determining whether violations of the Duke community standard had taken place. This type of adjudication requires time and care; the process rights of any accused must be protected, and that can lead to frustration—until you are the one who is accused. This type of work must be a part of maintaining the intellectual climate on campus, but it should not substitute for the actual intellectual dialogue that should be taking place. We desperately needed more and better speech on difficult topics to jumpstart our community. Some on campus were focused on the symbolic nature of the string of events, while others evaluated each incident independently, and focused on assigning individual blame for actions, or claiming that the acts were being perpetrated by campus outsiders which somehow made things better. Some students were frustrated that the university administration kept saying "this is not us" even though it kept happening by and to us, and requests from some students to better protect them from what they experienced as hate speech got louder.

I remained skeptical that Duke could do a good job of defining a list of words and symbols that could not be said, nor displayed on campus. Even more difficult would be dealing with the distinction between the intent of perpetrator and the experience of the attacked, and the process necessary to sort this out if we were to punish violations of Duke's community standard. I was worried that any attempt to fix things would create other problems and make things worse, and this was partly because the existing student judicial system did not even do its bread-and-butter mission of addressing cheating well, in my view and experience as a faculty member.

In November of 2018 I met with a group of students who wanted clarity about how students would be punished if they engaged in racially motivated hate speech. They pointed out that the Duke administration was comfortable keeping a broad and general policy that made "disruptive" protests unacceptable and punishable yet said there was no way they could navigate the same difficult to discern line with "racist" speech. This remained a good point and is a source of continued tension between some groups of students and the Duke administration. For me that meant we needed a new protest policy, not that we needed a speech code. That was not how this group of students saw it. They were continuing the conversation that the Commission on Hate and Bias had reported on to the community in 2016 but came down in a different place. They said they did not want to be protected from ideas, but from people who were using racist symbols to intimidate and make them feel like they did not belong at Duke. I said they were at Duke and did belong and we mostly talked past one another. I came into the meeting very much in agreement with the previous commission's warning that attempts to parse language ahead of time and set penalties would be very difficult for a university that had such an imperative to encourage more expression and speech. Even worse, some marginalized groups would be the most punished by attempts at devising such a system. My arguments were largely theoretical in nature or were supported with examples that were distant from my experience. The students who had come to talk with me had directly experienced racial attacks in the form of the word *nigger* written on their dorm door bulletin board, or had been told they did not belong at Duke. Or they were advocates of students attacked in these ways.

Discussions with students sharing their personal experiences helped me begin to understand the reality that racist hate speech has a disproportionate effect on people from groups that have historically been marginalized at places like Duke. Before I became chair of the Academic Council, my consideration of these issues was fully theoretical, and I had not personally ever felt limited in my ability to express myself on a college campus. These students experienced me as not being empathetic, and while that was not my intent, it was their experience.

At the AC conference room table over coffee and pastries in November, one of the students listened closely to me, though I had entered the room with my mind made up that a speech code was an unworkable bad idea. She waited patiently and said simply after I finished, Professor Taylor, you go home each night to your house, but I live in a dorm on campus. The word *nigger* has been used to enable the murder of Black people for centuries. I should be able to feel safe where I live. Someone who does not feel safe cannot participate in the dialogue and debate you describe at Duke.

Her response floored me in its clarity. I had neither listened well, nor managed much empathy for a group of students who had lived a very different experience from mine. This was not theoretical for them, as this slur had been written on *their dormitory door*. It was personal and went to their experience of being made to feel that they did not belong at Duke. This was not a singular incident, but a part of a pattern they experienced as students. There is no historical corollary of the word *nigger* that has been used against White people in the United States.

There just is not. I had only viewed the discussion of what to do about hate speech as an intellectual matter, which it is in part. However, these Duke students experienced a racial slur that had been written on *their dorm door bulletin board* as a threat to their physical safety, and an existential threat to the idea that they belonged at Duke. And not unreasonably given the history of how that word has been used. They were asking for the protection and sense of belonging that would provide them with the opportunity to join the academic fray that I claimed to want to defend. They wanted what I took for granted.

This conversation caused me to lose sleep, as well it should have. As I tossed and turned that night, I remembered participating in a racial healing circle as part of a training for leaders at Duke University during the summer of 2018. This approach was developed by Dr. Gail Henderson and was adapted at Duke University. These circles only work if conducted with a diverse group of people. Examples of prompts are, "What do you remember about your fifth birthday?" or "What is the first public news story that you remember?" These prompts get people talking about their lives and experiences without referencing race, and the ensuing discussion helps demonstrate connections, similarities, and differences in the group. The goal is to help participants see a bit of themselves in others who differ from them and to experience such a connection across racial identities. Race, at times, is explicitly discussed, while at other times it's not. The group determines the content.

The prompt that summer day was, "When have you felt like you have not been heard?" with a subsequent prompt of, "How did that make you feel?" There were two minutes allotted for group members to jot down their answers, and during this pause I could not think of what to write. "I have always felt heard, even though I may not have always gotten what I wanted" is a good summary of both my initial and considered reflection on the prompt. This made me anxious and did not seem like the correct thing to say, especially because others in the group were busily scribbling answers on index cards. I began thinking of times when the outcome I wanted did not come to pass, but as we moved into the discussion part of the circle the facilitator emphasized that this was not an outcome-driven question. I went with the truth and wrote my original reaction.

We went around the group with folks sharing times they had not been heard, and we discussed what people shared, asked questions, and kept moving. When it came my turn, I shared that I could not remember not being heard, and a Black woman in the group asked me a simple question in follow up: "Why do you think that you cannot think of a time?" and I answered that I think it was because I am a White man, who has a relatively prestigious job within the organization in which I work. This exchange led to more conversation, including other people who were White, noting instances in which they had not been heard, and a couple of relationships began that day continued after this training. My story was only my story. Telling the truth as you understand it in the scary area of talking about race can be an intervention because it is rare. We fear honesty and say what we think that we are supposed to say because we fear making a mistake and being punished in some manner.

I had slowly come to understand that we had three interrelated problems. First, the culture of debate and dialogue was not as robust as needed at Duke, especially outside of class. There was a paradox at work in which faculty enjoyed robust debate governed by professional norms in their field of expertise, but our students did not have the same for the many topics that are relevant to their lives. Second, faculty were increasingly crowded out of involvement in the campus culture of debate by professional staff and a plethora of outside speakers, and many of us (me) willingly focused on our own research. We need to re-engage. Third, we had a far more diverse community that needed to be formed into an academic culture, but we were too busy congratulating ourselves on the positive steps made in recruitment to ensure that the intellectual culture of the undergraduate student body was what we wanted and needed. Professional student affairs administrators are passionate advocates for the students, but on the whole are practitioners of what Jonathan Haidt and Greg Lukianoff have called "safetyism" in their 2018 book *The Coddling of the American Mind*. I think that at least part of why there has been such an explosion in the mental health needs among our students the past decade is our inability to form a more robust culture of free expression, debate and dialogue on campus that protects those who are attacked with more and better speech.

Enfolding 1,800 teenagers into an intellectual community required more explicit care than we applied, and we assumed too much. When I viewed students as wanting to be coddled by a speech code and to never have to think about something difficult is mostly a straw man creation of people like me who have never had to think much about our ability to speak up and participate when we wished. To some outside the university, students asking the university for protection and to uphold the student conduct code were labeled "snowflakes" or students who cannot bear to be exposed to new ideas. Sitting and chatting with them in a small group helped me to begin to understand that this characterization was incorrect. They were saying that they want the sense of belonging on campus that I take for granted *so that they can engage in discussing new ideas*. I regret that this clarity has only come to me in retrospect.

One Last Hurrah

As the Fall 2018 semester wound down, Vice President of Student Affairs Larry Moneta posted what became an online meme in Duke circles and perhaps more broadly. On his Facebook page, he posted "Several reasons to move to China. . .. . NOT" while he visited Duke Kunshan University. Dr. Moneta announced in September 2018 that he would retire at the end of the academic year in June 2019. His trip to visit Duke's campus in China was a valedictory of sorts. His posts were public and amplified by several student groups in China on Chinese social media, and in the United States on Facebook, and they were reasonably viewed as mocking Chinese culture. Especially hurtful was a picture of a squat toilet that Dr. Moneta had encountered on his trip. The vice president of student affairs at Duke University choosing to highlight such an image showed bad judgment in addition to cultural insensitivity. Squat toilets are present in some Duke campus buildings in China, but why would he choose to highlight this?

I was angry that for the second semester in a row, the same Duke leader had caused a racism-infused campus uproar. And this was not a matter of freedom of speech or expression. Dr. Moneta was and is free to write on his Facebook page what he wishes, but there were consequences to his exercise of that freedom. Since he was a vice president at Duke, it garnered more attention than it might otherwise have. And given the fiasco from the prior May in the campus coffee shop, it served to reignite that controversy. Most importantly, free expression risks showing others who you are and what you think. This unforced error showed a deep cultural imperialism on full display in a leader of a university that claimed to be a global university, a university that was going to remake liberal arts education in China. Bad judgment all around.

Dr. Moneta quickly announced that he was suspending his social media presence until the end of spring semester when he was set to retire. I assumed that the president and provost had insisted upon this step but did not know for sure. To be clear, I do not believe that Dr. Moneta set out to harm Duke with this post —I am confident he thought very little about the ramifications of posting several pictures that he thought were funny. Social media simply allows each of us the chance to demonstrate what is alive deep inside of us. There is a long-standing desire among the Allen Building leadership to name any racist event as a departure, a one-off, and not emblematic of the culture at Duke, but this is difficult to defend when such incidents continue to happen. It is more troubling and more truthful to acknowledge what is a part of each of us. And the only antidote is to practice talking openly about it; more speech, not less. Duke was stumbling to another semester break. Most notable about the incident was the speed with which the pictures spread and how rapidly the crisis brewed, and this was prescient of what would soon happen in the New Year.

I was ill-prepared by my two decades as a professor to think creatively about the balancing act required for a university to host a public facing intellectual culture because my career had focused on my own research. There was a paradox that was becoming clear —the individual disciplines did not have trouble debating difficult issues with a comity that understood the goal was developing knowledge. Our students did not enjoy the same. Faculty share rules about how to fight in an intellectual sense, and an expectation that all claims were not equally valid. This is because we share norms that determine when, how and why scholars in our field change their minds. However, it is far more difficult to create a campus wide community that vigorously discusses the many issues each day that students will face as citizens. But that is precisely what a university is supposed to do.

CHAPTER SIX: HOW LIBERAL FACULTY MAINTAIN RACIST SYSTEMS

Everything I ever thought has turned out different

CORMAC MCCARTHY, NO COUNTRY FOR OLD MEN

The faculty are the only comparative advantage that universities have—smart people who are allowed to seek their own intellectual interests within broad confines while being provided with resources to do so. The job at a place like Duke is focused, resourced creativity protected by academic freedom. This freedom has produced much intellectual fruit over time, across many fields of inquiry. The faculty are also the largest purveyors of racial harm at a university because of the power we have within an organization that values focused creativity. The academy's elevation of creativity, discovery and pushing the limits of understanding means that a great deal of faculty bad behavior has been overlooked for a long time. To change the university, you must change the faculty. And since the faculty have helped to create systems that operate by default in ways that create racial harm, change will be slow.

On January 26, 2019, as my term as Academic Council Chair entered its final semester, I got a text from an unrecognized cellphone telling me that a professor at Duke had discriminated against Chinese graduate students and that this treatment would harm Duke's reputation in China and around the world. The message included a link to what was claimed to be a social media website from China where, the anonymous person told me, the issue was being widely discussed. Later that evening I received a note from an anonymous Gmail account that levied charges of anti-Chinese discrimination in a master's degree program. The email included screenshots of two emails that contained the objectionable content. I read the emails and agreed that if they were real, the language contained in them would understandably be seen by students who are Chinese as discriminatory.

I went to bed knowing that I would need to confirm the authenticity of the emails before determining what to do next. By the time I got to my Academic Council office early the next morning, my email had blown up with reports of the original incident that had not only become a discussion item on Chinese social media, but in media outlets in the United States and around the world.

The emails were real, and the students and others were understandably upset because two senior faculty members had complained that students were speaking "Chinese" loudly in a break room in the department. The faculty found this to be rude, and had gone to the degree program director and asked for identifying information in the form of head shots of all the students in the program.

The implication that the students could be threatened with retaliation was confirmed explicitly in the email to all the students in the degree program. A portion of the email stated:

"Both faculty members replied that they wanted to write down the names (of the students speaking loudly) so they could remember them if the students ever interviewed for an internship or asked to work with them for a master's project."

There was immediate outrage, that was justified. The note was filled with so many culturally offensive notions (there is not a language called Chinese; English speakers hear Mandarin as loud because they do not understand it; and so on) as to nearly read as a caricature. When I first received a screenshot of the email, I assumed it was a hoax because it was cartoonishly bad. However, it was real and was sent by a Duke professor to the students in the degree program she directed.

I immediately saw a more complex situation that needed addressing, given my role representing the faculty at Duke. The assistant professor who sent the email was responsible for the message, as all of us are for our words, but there were numerous red flags in this note that identify the root problem as one of the culture in this department, and that meant the faculty—all of them, and not only the one who sent the email. While perhaps unclear to outsiders, the senior faculty in this department bore a great deal of responsibility for the culture that led a bright, up and coming assistant professor to think that this email was a good one to send. In fact, she likely felt that she had no choice but to follow the wishes of her senior colleagues who would be part of future reviews that would determine if and when she was promoted. That does not remove individual culpability from sending the email, but it helped to explain how deep the problem was in this department. This was more evidence that racism at Duke was not only a matter of Black and White.

The senior faculty hold the power in any academic department, and they had shirked their duty in this case in several ways. First, by placing a junior faculty member in the position of directing a master's degree program. Junior faculty should be getting their research and teaching careers launched instead of undertaking such profound service to a department. Second, they had a junior colleague do their dirty work. If they had a problem with the noise of a few graduate students, they should have spoken to them directly. Instead, they coerced their junior colleague and director of a graduate program to write all students in the program with a message that was bound to make students feel attacked and stereotyped. And the impact went well beyond one degree program. It was not only Mandarin speaking students who felt threatened. All international students would feel at risk on reading this email. Especially intimidating was that the faculty sought identifying information for the students so that they could remember them when the students sought research opportunities or asked for supervision of their thesis. That is retaliation. As chair of the AC, I began talking behind the scenes about this aspect of the case, raising concerns that senior faculty had put a junior colleague in this position at all, let alone pressured the junior colleague to send the email.

This is a classic example of structural racism playing out in an academic department. Note that it can be quite legitimate for a program to emphasize developing English language skills if that skill is relevant to the career aspirations of the students. But elevated faculty discomfort at not understanding a language is not a good reason to limit what language students speak on their own time in a common area of a department. There was a similar email sent in the same department the prior year that did not become public until it was repeated, underlining the structural nature of the problems in this department. This was not one rogue professor, but a messenger for the senior faculty, highlighting that the source of the problem was the shared department norms.

The junior faculty member resigned from her post as Director of the degree program and apologized along with the department chair, and the dean of the School of Medicine issued a statement affirming that students were free to speak whatever language they wished. She affirmed that such choices would not affect job recommendations or academic or research opportunities while they were in the degree program.

This was the end of the issue from Duke's perspective and the resignation quelled the crisis, but surviving a difficult news cycle is not the same thing as addressing structural racism on campus. This was simply a window into what had been a simmering issue for some time. The faculty who found the loud speaking of Mandarin objectionable, rude, and disrespectful, did not suddenly transform their perspective on the matter. A policy statement from the dean of the School of Medicine stated that the behavior that had been found objectionable by at least some faculty was acceptable to Duke. However, this papered over the reality that the faculty who created the culture of the department remained in their places of power, even if one assistant professor forever had her name associated with this incident. A public relations crisis was truncated, and Duke was ready to move on, though there was a group of students and faculty who sought to leverage this incident to expand the discussion of racism at Duke to include anti-Chinese and anti-Asian sentiment more broadly.

I replied to the concerned students' email and told them I was happy to have a conversation with them but preferred that we do so face to face. I did not want to engage in a back and forth by email with an anonymous group, though it was clear that they were at least linked in some way to the students in this program because they not only had the January 2019 email but one with similar content from 2018. I met with several students representing this group on two occasions, and we discussed a variety of issues, including items that were outside of my purview, such as an investigation of the incident by the Duke Office of Institutional Equity (OIE). A month after their initial email and meeting with me, they followed up noting that a month had passed and not enough had been done. I responded by email with a list of the things that had been done and others that were underway and told them to expect that change would be slower than they wished. I also noted that there was a key difference on campus in how individuals viewed the incidents. Some saw them as linked and suggestive of a broader problem with the campus culture, while others saw each incident as unique and isolated. We would have to improve our ability to talk about this to make headway as a community.

There was a lot of activity taking place behind the scenes. We discovered similar incidents of targeting specific groups of international students that had never become widely known. What emerged for me was a view of Duke that relied heavily on international students for tuition, especially in master's degree programs in numerous schools and departments yet did not have the culture that we needed to teach these programs well. We claimed to be a university of global excellence in both education and research, but there were numerous examples of quite hostile treatment of some of our international students. And while most incidents of this sort had an individual faculty or staff member who could be identified and blamed, the culture that created these incidents was ultimately a product of all of the faculty, who had the power to direct how to teach and how to treat students at an elite research university.

The following weeks of the spring semester, 2019, featured a great deal of focus on anti-Chinese racism. I learned a lot about another aspect of United States history that I had missed. It was clear that numerous Chinese students and Chinese American students felt excluded from different aspects of Duke's academic culture, or that they were singled out in different ways. Several faculty reminded me of the "Kappa Alpha Asia Prime" party that was held at Duke in 2013. This party had celebrated hyper-sexualized images of Asian women as being available to the fraternity brothers, an event that led to the fraternity being put on probation. Larger group discussions revealed that Chinese and Asian students had been targeted with a variety of discriminatory practices and harmed by the pervasive "model minority" image that many White people held to be true. This both stereotyped and pressured students to achieve at high levels just to be seen as 'average' Asian students. It was a trope that led to harm on campus.

When I met with several groups of students, they expressed a great deal of frustration that there had been so much focus on anti-Black racism. Faculty with research expertise in different aspects of China and other East Asian cultures, as well as the students themselves, were dismayed that some on campus found issues of anti-Chinese bias and discrimination to be a new one, given the long history from the Chinese Exclusion Act of 1882 to the present. The Chinese Exclusion Act suspended Chinese immigration to the United States, the only such law ever passed that named a specific group as having immigration rights fully suspended. This was done to protect jobs in the growing western part of the United States for people who were not Chinese—for cultural, religious, and economic reasons. But the bottom-line motivation was that people thought there were too many Chinese people in the Western part of the US. This view of immigrants was transactional: in the 19th century Chinese people were allowed to immigrate only when there were jobs that needed doing and no one else to do them. However, as workers began to make their homes in the United States, many in the White power structure wanted them to leave. Or at least to reduce immigration. This history was not well known on campus, including by me, and this led to a great deal of frustration and anger among students. Knowing this history helped to reinforce the global nature of the university and the system of higher education across the globe. I had a lot to learn, and it was not all Black and White.

Faculty Mentoring in My Department

Recruiting and mentoring junior faculty are among the most important tasks that senior faculty undertake, and we inevitably bring our biases—those that are good as well as those that are not. The Sanford School of Public Policy is my tenure home at Duke, and we have worked hard to recruit a more diverse faculty and to embed important concepts like racism and structural inequality in our curriculum. These topics need to be taught because they affect public policy outcomes and shape debates about tradeoffs in policy areas like education, health, transportation and energy. The Sanford School has long had disciplinary diversity among the faculty. Demographers, economists, historians, political scientists, psychologists, public health practitioners and scholars, and sociologists are represented on the faculty. That is an unusually broad disciplinary mix for one academic department in a university like Duke, and that brings both intellectual strengths and weaknesses. Strength because each discipline has something important to say about public policy, and they do so via different types of analytical methods. However, the broad intellectual diversity means that how faculty are judged for tenure differs in ways that can harm junior faculty because the senior faculty are often seeking to nudge the newbies toward our way of doing things. I think that has played a part in our having less success in keeping faculty at Duke after they get tenure, and at least part of the issue has been a failure of our mentoring culture as a department (if you asked 10 Sanford School Faculty about mentoring you would get 17 opinions, so remember, this is my story).

Losing faculty to other universities is a reality in a competitive academic ecosystem, and the only thing worse than losing a bright colleague to another university is having a bunch of faculty that no one else wants to recruit. That has not been my department's problem. In the last few years, we lost two junior faculty who are Black women to fellow Ivy Plus universities, and in both cases, I understood the logic of their decisions. Both colleagues had great options—stay at Duke or go where they did. However, we did not have a mentoring culture that maximized the chances that they would choose to remain at Duke after earning tenure. We faculty assumed that simply recruiting a more diverse faculty was all that we needed to do, and we thought little about how we mentored junior colleagues or how the broader culture at Duke influenced assistant professors as they developed their intellectual identity in Public Policy at Duke.

A few examples of what I mean.

In one case, a female faculty member of color was challenged in a classroom in an inappropriate fashion when a student shouted during class: "You do not know what you are talking about, you should not be teaching us." This was not a case of a student merely expressing a viewpoint. It was a White male student challenging the credentials and competence of a Black woman in front of a large class of students. The class assigned was an introductory course that I have taught numerous times. It's a challenging course for professors due to the breadth of the material, the reality that some students struggle generating a great deal of stress, and having to manage numerous teaching assistants to ensure that grading standards are fair across sections. The full professors discussed this incident and how to respond and we fully failed not only our colleague, but our students. We labeled the event as an episode allowed by freedom of speech and the academic freedom of the student who questioned our colleague's credentials. This was nonsense. It was instead a student who challenged the training of a female junior professor, and many of the students present felt the incident was about race. (It was about both race and gender in my view, understanding that all my information was second hand at best). And to be clear, the faculty member's Ph.D. was from an imminent university.

Let me just say that I have never been challenged by a student in that way, but if I were I would throw them out of the class for the rest of that day. *Not if they challenged an idea, a theory, or a statement of fact that I made*, but if they shouted you are not well trained and do not know what you are talking about.

It is important for me to reiterate that the full professors discussed this incident, and that meant that I knew about it, expressed anxiety and uncertainty about it, but I did not press hard enough. I let it pass, to be handled by another faculty member, whose job it was to do so. We as a faculty chose to de-escalate the situation by calling it something that it was not, and in doing so, we failed our junior colleague, our students, and ourselves. Later on, she left for another university, not because of this incident in and of itself, but because it was a canary in the coal mine of our faculty culture of mentoring junior faculty.

Another example demonstrates how difficult it can be to well-mentor a colleague who brings different methodological approaches to common topics. My department has a team-based mentoring approach whereby a junior faculty member is assigned to a primary mentor supported by two others, and they together form a mentoring committee. These faculty work with junior colleagues to talk about their academic career. Should the faculty member write a book, or three journal articles? Should a project that requires primary data collection be undertaken, or delayed until after tenure due to the more speculative and difficult nature of such research? How should the junior colleagues emerging interests and intellectual development shape the direction of their research and teaching? Should the faculty member write a grant to fund research if it is a long shot to receive? And so on.

I was a member of one such mentoring committee more than a decade ago for a junior colleague of color whose research focused on the impact of racism and structural inequality on health and public policy outcomes. These were the precise topics that we as a faculty had decided should be integrated into our curriculum because of their impact on human health, and we recruited a rising star with research and teaching expertise in those areas. A mentoring committee always faces a fine line dilemma of guiding a junior scholar toward a path that maximizes their chance to obtain tenure and solidifies their research career, without changing the scholarship of the colleague merely to fit the committee's interests. *This is a very difficult line to navigate in such an interdisciplinary academic department.* This is where the benefit of having an intellectually diverse department as measured by discipline and methodology can make tasks like mentorship more difficult.

In meeting after meeting, well-meaning liberal, White faculty sought to transform the interests of this scholar into one who published more in line with their own work. I know because I was one of them. We had collectively said that we wanted more diversity not only in the demographics of the faculty, but of the topics studied and the way that they were studied. For example, this scholar joined three types of analysis to study health outcomes: qualitatitve data collection and analysis; large scale secondary data analysis; and the use of biological markers such as telomeres to approximate cell age. We said that we wanted a new approach to the old issue of differential health outcomes by race, but we did not seem to mean this when push came to shove. Instead we tried to shape this junior colleague in ways that would produce scholarly output we better understood. We did worse than congratulating ourselves for success in recruitment, we sought to change our colleague into something that made him unrecognizable to himself, and misaligned with his talents, and desires. He earned tenure despite our collective efforts to mentor him. Again, I say this as a member of the mentorship committee—I participated in our collectively messing up.

Progressive, liberal-minded faculty are the most consistently powerful conduits of racism at Duke University, even as they fully reject racism as an ideology. We fail to see it embedded in our own lives. I know this to be true because I have learned to see this in myself. For example, in the late 1990s, when I was a new junior faculty member at Duke, I strode across the main campus quad during the first week of classes and said hello to a student who attended my class on the first day. We engaged in brief, polite banter until I asked the student, "What position do you play on the football team?" He looked embarrassed and said that he did not play football and that he was not an athlete. I stammered out something, but what I had clearly communicated to this fit Black male student was that I assumed the only way he could be at Duke was to be a football player. My goal had been to greet one of my students in a casual campus setting in a welcoming manner, but in fact I had communicated that he did not fully belong at Duke because he was Black. My intent had not been to harm him, but my intentions had no effect on his experience of my actions. There was no opportunity for me to follow up because the student dropped the class, and I cannot say that I blame him.

CHAPTER SEVEN: TALKING AND DOING

Everyone has a plan until they get punched in the mouth

MIKE TYSON

On July 1, 2019 I became the Director of the Social Science Research Institute (SSRI), one of five signature institutes at the university with responsibilities that spanned all ten schools at Duke, from the School of Medicine to the School of Divinity. The opportunity to support scholarly research and open discussion of social science adjacent topics on campus was invigorating. I saw a great opportunity for Duke to leverage our location in the American South as a center for excellence in scholarship on race (which we were and are), as well as to learn to talk about it as an intellectual community (a work in progress). Research on the American South necessarily includes but is not limited to race and racism, and there was interest among some Duke leaders for the university to move in this direction. However, others were skeptical and thought this would limit our ability to be a global university. I took the post of Director knowing that I would have to make the case for why this shift would enhance our standing as a global university, as well as face the difficult task of reorienting budget flows within an existing bureaucracy. That task is never easy.

Discussing intellectual priorities fused with budgetary reality was a return to more normal intellectual leadership at the university for me. The chair of the Academic Council must frame their public speech to seek, align with and amplify group consensus. There is acute focus on process. However, as Director of an Institute whose mission clearly includes elevating scholars in fields relevant to the topics of the day, I was able to speak out more clearly and boldly.

I wanted to stimulate a conversation about racism on campus for the 2019-20 academic year that was not initiated by a high-profile racist incident, so I wrote an op-ed piece in the first issue of the *Duke Chronicle* on August 20, 2019 semester entitled "What is Wrong at Duke: White Supremacy is the Root." My goal was to shift the intellectual conversation toward our faculty expertise in race and racism, and to do so before a racist incident grabbed campus attention. I pointed to my colleague Eduardo Bonilla-Silva, a James B. Duke Professor of Sociology, who wrote the seminal academic work on structural Racism, *Racism Without Racists*, in 2002. Starting the conversation before there was a specific incident might help us to proceed as scholars and not only be reactive to the particular facts of an incident.

Looking back at my August 2019 piece in 2025, several things stand out. First, it seems like a lifetime ago given that it was the start of an academic year that would be disrupted by COVID. Second, there is language that I used in good faith that I would not use today. For example, the phrase White supremacy was a jarring part of the op-ed, but now it is often seen as performative when used by White writers, and I tend to shy away from it. The point was that racism is a problem that is broader than a group of people marching around chanting 'blood and soil' as they did in Charlottesville, Va. in 2017. *There is a problem beyond those people.*

The book *White Fragility* would not figure in my argument today because there are better books on the subject that I have now read. However, you only get to live your life through the windshield, looking ahead and moving forward. And that book was a part of my personal journey that continues. We are all in progress and if you are so bold as to write what you think, the internet will remember. The ensuing campus discussion of my piece ranged from "thank you" to "how could you" to "you went to UNC and want to hurt Duke" but on balance I am not sure that there was any appreciable effect on the campus culture of discussion and debate. Maybe it was simply arrogance that made me think that I could initiate such a discussion. What I had done was roll a bomb into the room with no pre-warning, and no real plan to channel energy for better communication, debate and dialogue. Perhaps I was simply managing my own anxiety about what it meant to lead at that time on campus. Managing my own anxiety is a thread that runs through my time as a campus leader, and it is something that I continue to work on.

Around the same time that piece appeared, a long time SSRI employee told me that there were "Black people jobs and White people jobs at SSRI and Duke," in response to my asking about his career goals. He sensed my surprise and quickly added, "Someone who knows us both told me that I could trust you," and that first conversation jumpstarted our relationship. Why I was surprised is less clear because this is exactly the type of structural racism that Professor Bonilla-Silva had written about two decades before. Still, the plain language and certainty in his statement was jarring to me personally, just as what I wrote in the newspaper was jarring to some White people who reached out. I was saved by a plain-speaking colleague from the stereotypical faculty error of focusing on the theoretical in lieu of seeing its practical manifestation right before my eyes. To focus on research that describes the existence of systems of racial harm, while not addressing the one for which I was now responsible, would be ironic. This conversation-as-intervention forced me to slow down and think about being responsible for the overall culture and the well-being of each employee working for SSRI. You cannot change what an organization does without paying attention to the human beings who work there. This is obvious to me now but was not then. My view of the organization had been to see it as a monolith that could be reoriented to meet the needs of the university. My understanding had to be updated.

My experience as a leader at Duke has included many high-profile discussions and disagreements, with me commonly playing the role of devil's advocate, or suggesting ideas with virtually no chance of coming to pass, in an attempt to push the leadership culture of Duke administrators and the Board of Trustees. I was comfortable in the mix of intellectual give and take, and the discretion required of this type of leadership. However, it was not the same thing as leading an organization that has specific daily tasks to execute. Daily tasks equals people, and people mean conflict, and conflict means pain. And racism was an important part of the story. I tasked the deputy director of SSRI, a trusted colleague with more personal loyalty to me than he did to protecting the SSRI bureaucracy, with investigating the issue of "White people jobs and Black people jobs." His knowledge of Duke mixed with an "outsider" perspective of SSRI was invaluable in helping me to identify staff who felt that their opportunities had been improperly limited. We focused on racism but not solely.

By Christmas of 2019, it was clear that several staff who identified as Black had experienced a lack of advancement or were unhappy and felt stuck in their jobs. Some were certain that racism was a key part of the problem, others less so, but there was plenty to worry about even in the idiosyncratic, individual trajectories of the staff. Systems, structures, and assumptions can serve to hold some people out of job advancement opportunities while helping others to move forward. There need not be an individual or individuals setting out to harm people of color for racial bias to be operating within an organization. Just as my intention had no impact on the experience of the student I assumed to be a football player, Black staff could be harmed even if no one set out to achieve this outcome.

The deputy director and I talked with staff colleagues who identified as Black about our concerns and jointly devised plans to help them seek other opportunities at Duke or beyond if they wished. One employee returned to graduate school, and two others transitioned to jobs in other parts of Duke, assisted by me and the deputy director, who had a huge network of colleagues in the School of Medicine. Since SSRI was in budget cutting and staff layoff mode (I assumed the post knowing that I would have to make large, difficult cuts to the organization, as directed by the then-Provost Sally Kornbluth), there were few internal opportunities for advancement at the time. However, one staff member did move into a new position within SSRI before transitioning to a promotion in a different unit at Duke a few years later. I had been too quick to focus only on the intellectual transition issues, and my most important contribution may have been nudging the internal culture of the organization to looking to identify and change systems of bias. This remains a work in progress, especially given the hybrid work shifts that took place due to the COVID pandemic.

Anything that is important for a university to change has to be led by the faculty, its most important asset and only comparative advantage. This was how I determined where to invest my time and SSRIs fungible resources after we had undertaken required budget cuts and addressed internal culture issues. We changed the Bass Connections theme hosted by SSRI to Race and Society, and selected Tyson Brown, a rising star sociologist whose research focuses on structural racism and its impact on health and thriving. This shifted SSRI resources toward the study of race and society by default, because seven to ten faculty-led projects that enfold undergraduate and graduate students on research teams will focus on race annually for the next five to seven years. This is not an individual or a committee making grand statements about Duke and its culture, but faculty engaging their scholarly expertise in research and teaching alongside students. The reason a university exists.

I got another key opportunity to shape the curriculum at Duke by participating in developing the first in a series of "University 101" course offerings. We (I, Kerry Haynie, Aimee Kwon, and Charmaine Royal) created a course entitled "The Invention and Consequences of Race" in Fall 2021 and enrolled around ninety Duke undergraduates. The University 101 courses were designed to provide undergraduates with an introduction to large societal issues in a "big ideas" type of format, taken early in their college career. This allows students an opportunity to follow up and dig deeper into the material in a given area. In 2022 a similar course was created that focused on climate change, in 2023 one on artificial intelligence debuted, in 2024 one focused on the digital life of humans, and so on. But the race course has continued to be offered each academic year by different faculty.

The course was developed because of a confluence of faculty interests and expertise within the university, fueled by new resources from the university. The goal of this course was to provide students with a scholarly overview of the concept of race, focusing on the United States but with some comparative materials from other nations, with specific topics being taught by faculty with expertise in those areas. We included experts from Duke who had given their life's work to understanding race as a concept and how human understanding of it has changed over time and across cultures, and to what effect. We also selected guest speakers from other universities and organizations who likewise were domain experts and had been engaged in research and teaching on the concept of race long before Duke University declared that developing an anti-racist culture was a priority.

The Duke Magazine did an exposé of this course in the spring, 2023 issue of the magazine that was mailed to alums and Professor Kerry Haynie, then chair of the Department of Political Science, said this about the course:

"When it was time to create the UNIV 101: The Invention

and Consequences of Race, Professor Kerry Haynie had an issue. The course came about as part of Duke's anti-racism effort, and Haynie's central concern was simple: "I don't know what people mean by anti-racist," he said. "I mean, I think I have an idea of what they think they mean."

"But I don't know how to do that. That is not what I do as an academic."

A journalist interviewing the lead professor of the first University 101 course on race would assume that since the course flowed out of the university's commitment to create an anti-racist culture, that this concept would be central to the course. What was going on?

The faculty who developed the course were happy to have the extra resources needed to create it but were not going to be bound by the language used by the university to describe it. This highlights the prerogatives of the faculty who hold the academic freedom to develop a course as their expertise dictates. This is a bedrock principle of the university that demonstrates the independent nature of the faculty and provides an example of the limits of university leaders to move forward with initiatives that do not have the support of at least some of the faculty. Especially in a high-profile area where the university has numerous faculty experts, it is a big mistake for a university leader to proceed without the explicit input and support of the faculty, who can lead from their research and scholarship.

We handled this uncertainty by talking about it openly in class, and in how we discussed the initiative with our faculty colleagues across the campus. We went toward the tension and disagreement about what belonged in a course such as this one. This class was the antithesis of what conservative activists would imagine when they heard there was a university course about race. It never made Fox News or anything of that nature because the class was an academic treatment of the study of race, students brought numerous perspectives on the material, and they handled the dialogue around difficult topics well. It is not inevitable that a university course on race would be constructed in this way but it is clearly possible and what I would expect from faculty: an introduction to the scholarly research on race.

There is an important discussion to be held about respecting the line between scholarship, research, and advocacy. It is faculty who most commonly step over this line, and when they do so, it rightly causes consternation. We bent over backward not to do this, which is why we had faculty focus on their life's work, condensed into one week in the course. Careful, cautious, building upon past work, naming questions for others to answer. It turned out when the academy functions as intended, it is often boring for those who simply want a sound bite to match their prior beliefs.

Developing the course took a great deal of time and energy because there were so many sub-topics and ways to proceed. There were disagreements among the faculty involved. (Not only the four of us who constructed the final syllabus and offered the course, but there were approximately fifteen others who had input.) We disagreed about what belonged in the course and what did not, whether one had to agree that building an anti-racist culture at Duke was a good idea, or even whether we knew what that meant, and so on. Internally, the committee wrestled with the desire to feature a breadth of disciplines that studied race, constrained by the 15-week semester schedule and the need for weekly presentation of materials. There were faculty we consulted who felt we excluded relevant topics. For example, a Classics/Old Testament scholar from the Department of Religion felt that we should have included a week on the use of race in premodern literature to demonstrate how old the idea of race is. There simply was not enough time to cover everything. Similarly, there was tension around navigating the line between scholarship and advocacy, and we had good discussions about both the presence of such a line and how to identify and navigate it with numerous faculty as we developed the course and prepared for each week's class and materials. Talking with the students about this line was a key part of the course. Even if some faculty disagreed about where it lay, we acknowledged that there was a difference between scholarship and advocacy.

COVID, and Nothing New Under the Sun

The COVID pandemic fully upended the world, while revealing nothing new about racism at Duke and beyond. When Spring Break 2020 was extended from one to two weeks to give the university time to adapt to our new reality, there was a string of "nevers" that became "until nows" that solidified into "new normals." How the university operated on a day-to-day basis with work from home and online classes was unrecognizable to the reality at Duke just a few weeks before. Duke's speed in adapting to online functioning for classes and research during the last six weeks of the spring semester was astonishing. And changes that would have taken committee after committee for approval were made via email to all the faculty from the provost. Another example of rapid adaptation was Duke allowing PhD dissertation defenses to be conducted fully on ZOOM, a practice that was forbidden before the pandemic, when all members of the faculty committee had to be present in person.

My wife and I recall fondly the return of our three adult children for around ninety days at the beginning of the pandemic —it had been a decade since all five of us had been together in the same house for so long. It was a terrible situation with a definite silver lining. Each child had their bedroom, and our house has a basement so there was plenty of space to spread out. During that time one of our kids finished college, the other his freshman year in college, and the third worked from home along with my wife and myself. We ordered food to be delivered, and when we shopped in the grocery store, we had N95 masks to wear. We managed to construct a life that was at least insulated and isolated from the risks of COVID. However, the people working in the grocery stores were not, nor were those in gas stations, food delivery workers, and the like. Workers in these areas were transformed from being people in "low wage jobs" or "service industry jobs" to "essential workers" like nurses, doctors, firefighters, police, nursing home workers and caregivers. All of these fellow citizens bore a disproportionate burden from COVID because their jobs put them in harm's way, and in Durham there was a clear race gradient in such work; Black people and those identifying as Hispanic were much more likely to be working in those jobs than were Whites. This led inevitably to racial differences in COVID infections, hospitalizations, and deaths.

Structural advantages to Whites and structural disadvantages to those who were not White are nothing new at Duke or in Durham, but they were put on full display in a new way by the summer of 2020, and there was more acknowledgment of these persistent realities by people who were White. This was particularly the case in my neighborhood where I spent far more time than I did before the pandemic. My neighborhood is reliably liberal in voting patterns, and there was a sense that we had not fully understood how structural racism worked until COVID.

Similarly, the pandemic did not create inequalities among students, but did underline them. One student in my class finished the semester from home with no wi-fi and participated from the parking lot of a McDonalds where she could get a free Wi-Fi signal. Because campus housing closed, another student had no place to go, much less a large house in which to ride out the pandemic; he slept in his car for two days until Duke University stepped in with emergency housing support. Duke has enjoyed success in diversifying the student body, especially with respect to students from lower income backgrounds, but the pandemic exposed the knife's edge on which some students' families were living. It quickly became apparent that classes were an important community connection for students, so we commonly spent the first fifteen to twenty minutes checking in on one another throughout April 2020 as the semester wound down. One of the tips that professors had been provided about online education was that we should require students to have their video cameras on throughout the class period, something that I sought to enforce rigidly until one student in the class reached out and said that they did not want other students to see the place they were staying during the pandemic. They were living on a relative's couch and did not have a private place in which to participate in class. These stories were not perfectly correlated with race, but they were correlated. Students of color were disproportionately affected by these challenges as compared to students in my class who identified as White.

On Friday May 22, 2020, I co-hosted a joint SSRI/Duke School of Medicine Center for Translation Science Institute webinar with Dr. Ebony Boulware, who is now the dean of the Wake Forest School of Medicine. The event focused on the impact of the COVID pandemic on vulnerable communities, and brought together faculty, staff, and students along with community partners to reflect on what had come to pass and how we as a community (Duke and Durham) should move forward in addressing the pandemic. This webinar explained how the patterns of illness and death due to COVID mirrored existing inequalities in housing, income, education, and access to health care and jobs. The same patterns were simply being expressed in a new way through COVID infection, morbidity, and death. The language of Social Determinants of Health was used to highlight the multi-factor nature of racial groups and their different rates of COVID, serious illness, and death. It was not race per se that led to an increase in infection, but that race was associated with having jobs that put workers at risk, often without access to the best personal protective equipment. Or it was associated with living in crowded housing, with reduced resources to protect themselves. Or it was associated with being more likely to be uninsured. This pattern was expected and not surprising to experts, but it was a new insight for many people in my neighborhood and church.

I had a foot in both worlds, and the difference in

understanding the pandemic floored me. I was at a loss for what to say when it came time for my summary comments at the end of the day that were supposed to focus on the next steps for research after a class. I said this (transcript lightly edited):

"I've had a pit in my stomach for most of the day due to the disconnect between the experts who are not surprised by the inequality—the unequal death and morbidity that we've seen because there's very much been a sense of, we've seen this movie before. At the same time and in parallel there is a cultural discourse that seems real and inquisitive. I agree the media has led the way in asking questions and pointing out how much more likely Black Americans are to die than White Americans from COVID. The pit in my stomach comes from the dual nature of my existence in multiple communities."

This was basic stuff so far as epidemiologists and public health experts were concerned (my Ph.D. is in Public Health), but there were questions being raised afresh in other parts of my life. "There must be some genetic predisposition" or "those folks must not wear masks" were common explanations masquerading as questions to explain different death rates by race due to COVID. Most people had not thought much about health inequalities. It did seem that my White neighbors, family members and non-public-health colleagues wanted to find a biological answer or an explanation that put the responsibility solely on the person who got sick. I felt discouraged as the Memorial Day weekend began. I would soon feel worse.

Fleeting Moment of Racial Reckoning

On Memorial Day, 2020, and just three days after the conference at Duke, George Floyd was murdered by a Minneapolis police officer who detained him in a choke hold for more than eight minutes. He suffocated in the view of several dozen people, all of this caught on a cell phone video. This horrific event has been well-covered and ignited a short window of racial reckoning across the nation. It was during that time (June 2020) that President Price announced Duke's commitment to developing an anti-racist culture, which financed the development of the University 101 course on race.

There were other horrific examples of racially motivated violence on display during the weeks before Memorial Day, and with people at home watching television, these incidents also helped ignite the moment. Looking back at my email account the week following Mr. Floyd's death shows how present and urgent the discussion was among friends, acquaintances, and church members outside of my research and public policy colleagues at Duke.

On Thursday, May 28, 2020, my pastor, a White man who was in his mid-60s wrote me the following email with the subject heading "Killing":

"So, what would you do if you were in the crowd watching the police kill a man? Sure, one assumes that the police are not going to kill a man. But I feel like I should at least practice using the video on my phone as quickly as possible. Also, that I should stop and observe anytime I see police doing the most routine thing with a Black person."

This was not necessarily performative grandstanding among White folks, of which there was undoubtedly some; it might also have been heartfelt anguish and discovery, acknowledgment and understanding. It may have been deferred, but it was not too late. For a brief period, the focus of discussion among my White liberal and progressive friends was not to simply blame Donald Trump for racism, but to look more closely at U.S. history and the ideas that were written into our own hearts and minds; to look at ourselves. President Trump had indeed normalized talking out loud about race and racism for political advantage by saying things that for decades had only been whispered. However, we would never address these issues on Duke's campus simply by pointing fingers at others. We would have to heal ourselves, from the inside out and the Summer of 2020 seemed like the start of something new and important.

CHAPTER EIGHT: MASS PRODUCING DEI TRAINING

The idea of a mass audience was really an invention of the Industrial Revolution

DAVID CRONENBERG

Large organizations need measurable activities that can be tracked as they seek to achieve publicly stated goals. The C Suite of a Fortune 500 company is responsible to their Board, shareholders and customers to follow through on such commitments. A university is accountable to an even larger group of stakeholders, each of whom have different types of relationships with the organization: faculty, staff, students, alums, fans, taxpayers and society as a whole, but without the predictable quarterly earnings report faced by a publicly traded company. Universities have a more diffuse group of interested parties, and they lack the clarifying reality of a clear bottom line of profit and loss to manage toward. However, the biggest difference between a university like Duke and a Fortune 500 corporation is the faculty, and it is useful to understand our role in attempts to address racism through mass produced DEI.

Universities and Fortune 500 companies adopted DEI commitments and developed related programming in the aftermath of the COVID 2020 Summer and both have at least partly turned away from this commitment by the Spring of 2025. There is an inevitable tradeoff between granular, incremental and slow change that may be more meaningful, and the need of leaders to say that they are following through on commitments. And people want accountability for leaders. When corporations determined there would be changes in hiring practices for executive jobs and an expansion of mandated training, those things took place or company leaders got fired. A member of Duke University's Board of Trustees who is a business executive asked me a few years back why it was so difficult for the university to carry through with long-stated goals of hiring a more diverse faculty (pre COVID). Why didn't we just get on with it? I told him that the big difference between Duke and large corporations is the faculty who serve as a conservatizing force who are not only entrenched following tenure, but who bring a base conservatism to what they most care about, their research. Anyone can be fired in a corporation, and the standard is whether their actions have helped improve the profit/loss math. The focus in the corporate world is short term, and in academia, long term. There are benefits and drawbacks to both.

Exasperated, he followed up. "But don't faculty want a more diverse faculty?" he asked. Yes, in many or perhaps even most cases we do, *but we do not see ourselves as needing any help determining who to hire and we see ourselves as incapable of racial harm because we view ourselves as enlightened,* thus faculty resent any encroachment on our prerogatives, or activities that pull us away from our research and teaching.

It is a sociological fact that faculty are more liberal than average as measured by voter registration and survey responses, so it is surely a paradox that the modern university is the most conservative institution in the United States, precisely because of the faculty. Forget about how we vote. What we care most about is our research, and in this area we do tomorrow what we did today and yesterday, primarily because of how academic disciplines operate to produce knowledge. The null hypothesis of no effect of an intervention explicitly preferences the status quo, by default, in true conservative fashion. *You must move beyond existing knowledge to make your mark in academe. It is difficult to identify something new* and that is precisely what faculty give their professional lives to. One has to earn the truth of an argument via the rules of a discipline, and a finding that is new today will be the one overturned tomorrow by new evidence. These statements may seem like utter nonsense from outside the academy, but you must understand their elemental truth if you wish to bring about changes on a college campus.

At a place like Duke, if the faculty changes, so too will the university. Similarly, if we do not change, it will not. This conservatism is neither good, nor bad. It is a fact.

Further, faculty tend to be more vitally linked with and beholden to our intellectual discipline and research interests than to a given university. However, after tenure, we can typically remain at the university where we received tenure as long as we do our job (research, teaching, service). Tenure was and is designed precisely as a conservatizing force in the academy, to ensure that entire fields could not be done away with on a whim, and to ensure that scholars proceed using the evidentiary standards of their discipline and not what their Dean or the government wants them to conclude. This is why it was far easier for Fortune 500 companies to move lock, stock and barrel toward DEI programming than it was for universities like Duke. By the fall of 2020, large corporations decided that DEI was good business and moved forward with training, statements, and new approaches. However, faculty remained skeptical both of their need for training and the utility of the time required for same.

Duke Faculty Pushback Prior to Supreme Court Decision

Upon receiving an email in May 2022 about a mandatory training sent to all students, faculty and staff in his department, a distinguished virologist committed one of the most dreaded acts imaginable in the academy: he hit "reply all" to an email that had many recipients.

"My initial reaction is that I refuse to engage in left-wing Maoist political propaganda workshops, and as a tenured faculty member, that is my choice," he wrote after receiving the department-wide email, according to the Duke Chronicle, the student newspaper, which stated that the paper had reviewed the email chain.

This occurred more than a year before the June 2023 Supreme Court decision that ruled unconstitutional the use of race in undergraduate admissions, an event that was certainly a tipping point for the pushback and reversal of DEI momentum nationally in both business and higher education. However, it demonstrates that the assumed uniformity of the faculty for expanded DEI training was incorrect. For every public incident at Duke, there were many more grumblings behind the scenes about DEI training, especially given that it was additive on top of the many other trainings required at a research university, especially for those who conduct research with human subjects.

I do not know the specific training that was being required of everyone in the distinguished professor's department, but his email is an example of how tenured faculty can and do throw their weight around in sometimes unreasonable ways, and this behavior has a disproportionate impact on others, especially those with less power. In my experience, faculty lashing out in such a manner is often triggered by issues related to race and especially to efforts to combat racism in the academy via DEI training. This is an example of how and why faculty are responsible for a disproportionate amount of racial harm on campus, regardless of their intent. There is often a gap between intent and the impact of words spoken by someone with disproportionate power. I do not believe this faculty member's email was racist. However, it is easy to imagine that a student, staff member, or junior faculty member with less power feeling intimidated knowing this influential scholar felt strongly enough about the training to write everyone in the department. I want to be clear that I am not saying that this professor's email was racist, nor do I believe that was his intent.

Second, and of most concern to me, he badly misstates the nature of academic freedom—it is not a license to do anything that you wish, nor to refuse activities that Duke University as an employer can legally require (at least it could in 2022). Tenure is the granting of academic freedom to enable a scholar to pursue one's intellectual passions, commonly in a narrow and discrete field, without fear of reprisal. That is not at stake when the university requires training for a faculty member. "And this is my right as a tenured faculty member" were his exact words as recorded in the student newspaper. He directly invokes tenure as shielding him from training. He could not be more wrong legally, his thinking was sloppy, and he equated academic freedom with his own preferences, regardless of topic. This trivializes academic freedom as the crucial protection of the pursuit of knowledge that it is. This shows that we faculty need to spend more time thinking about these fundamental concepts that are central to the university. In this faculty member's defense, he used his time at Duke to do the research that made him a distinguished scientist, and likely never felt his ability to speak in the ways of his discipline as being at risk so he had little incentive to think about it.

My final thought is an uncomfortable one for me: the explosion of training at Duke and beyond following the Summer of 2020 might have made things worse, even before the political backlash that ensued. Again, there is a big difference between intent and effect. And there is tremendous variation in the relevance and quality among trainings that I have taken and helped to develop or test at Duke (not only in DEI, but also in human subjects training that primarily focuses on human subjects rules in 45 CFR 46).

There are good DEI training courses that I have completed at Duke. For example, the Anti-Semitism 101 seminar offered by the university through the Freeman Center for Jewish life is excellent, and I was intellectually stimulated to read two books as a follow up. This is the best that training can offer, not only providing guidelines and tools, but sparking an interest that begins a process of self-directed learning. There are also some truly bad trainings that are a waste of time. For example, prior to the pandemic when I was still chair of the Academic Council, Duke began offering an equity scholars training program. This course offered faculty the opportunity to learn how to improve their teaching with a goal of being more equitable in how they did so. The stated goal was to help faculty improve their ability to help all students in their classes reach their potential, and it focused on barriers to this outcome. Several faculty members reached out to me complaining about how simplistic and rote the training was, and the faculty were mad that their time was being wasted. I investigated by reading the curriculum and completing some of it online and had to agree with my colleagues. This was a canned offering commonly used for high school teachers and had been adapted for the college setting. It was not an effective tool for Duke faculty because it did not engage them where they were, it was not worth their time, and these were faculty who had applied for the opportunity to take the course. They wanted to learn how to be better teachers for all students in their increasingly diverse classes. This was a disastrous waste of time and money, and the program was greatly changed, as it should have been.

Conservatism of faculty

Most Chairs want to be Deans, who want to be Provosts who want to be Presidents. And they typically must bring about change via new initiatives to demonstrate their worth as academic leaders. This often produces faculty hiring in a new area, or an emphasis within a strength, and the existing faculty serve as a conservatizing force against such changes for two reasons. First, because of the intellectual conservatism of methods of research procedure across fields. They differ in specifics, but in all cases, new ideas must make the case via evidence that a given discipline acknowledges. So, faculty will always be skeptical of new ideas that are outside of their narrow intellectual interests and methods. And second, because faculty wield tremendous power in implementing hiring plans once a given position is approved by university leaders. At Duke, the Provost and Deans ultimately approve hiring plans, and academic departments can be winners or losers, as can particular fields within them. In my tenure home of the Sanford School of Public Policy, our discussions about "breadth v focus" in terms of public policy area (education, health, development, etc.) are legion. The instant that there is an emerging consensus to hire more in area A, faculty in areas B, C and D typically join forces against the change. As I have heard former Duke Provost Peter Lange say several times in a warm-up joke during an introduction to a talk, "Provosts are like caretakers of cemeteries. There are many people under each, but none of them are listening to anything I say."

Faculty most consequentially wield their power in three- to four-person committees that are given the task of undertaking a search, interviewing candidates, bringing them to campus for interviews, and then writing a report that recommends a course of action for hiring to a faculty department, chair or Dean. Centralized leadership plays a key role in determining the discipline and department of where faculty will be hired in a given year, and the Dean and Provost ultimately make the hiring decisions, but faculty are assigned the responsibility of wading through applications to develop a short list. There is tremendous power in this curating role.

The last hiring committee I served on had several hundred applications for one post. I read every application including published papers or dissertation chapters for the top 25 or so candidates that the committee agreed upon. We then reduced the list to a dozen who got zoom interviews, and finally, we brought in three candidates for two-day campus visits and finally made a recommendation on hiring to the faculty, who could vote to approve or deny our report. The considered judgment of the faculty went to the Dean and Senior Associate Dean to make the final determination and to make an offer of employment and negotiate a contract. It makes me tired re-reading the above paragraph. And the Dean and Provost can buck the faculty judgement, but that is a provocative step given the time the faculty put into the search, and this is a power typically used sparingly.

The point is that it is a slow and laborious process to hire new faculty, and that is a conservatizing force in a university. When we hire new faculty, we are not only getting a new scholar and teacher, but we are adding someone with whom we might have to share lunch for two decades. It is the politically liberal faculty, who bring the conservative impulse to the enterprise, in part because long after a Provost has moved on to be a President elsewhere, faculty will still be sharing lunch with the faculty hired under the last Provost's new initiative. And a faculty member is first and foremost in a Department and not simply "at Duke."

Faculty are often seen as hegemonic from the outside, and especially by conservative critics who focus on political party registration or surveys of ideology. This leads to a caricature of the faculty from outside the academy is that we are a bunch of woke warriors executing a grand conspiracy to indoctrinate today's youth in our DEI dreams. In fact, we faculty can barely conspire to have lunch, largely because we understand ourselves to be the ultimate free agents. It is often the case that faculty tend to agree about most matters of voting choices that are available (Kamala Harris v. Donald Trump), but if we managed to get together for lunch and agreed about 98% of the topics discussed, we would spend most of our time hotly debating the other 2%. Faculty are independent, focused on their own opportunity and success, often underestimate the importance of others on their success and first and foremost have benefited from the existing system if they are tenured, making them slow to participate in its change. This conservatism is as intended, though it clearly brings plusses and minuses to the university.

I have been searching for an analogy and have one that will make everyone mad.

Faculty are more like professional golfers than any other profession, and vice versa. Professional golf is exceedingly competitive, with access to tournaments depending upon results. The better you play, the more you can play. Alternatively, if you play poorly, you cannot enter tournaments and therefore not make a living. If you lose your PGA Tour card, you have to get another job, or start over at a lower level golf tour. Similarly, there are commonly hundreds of applications for each assistant professor opening at Duke. And whomever gets a job as an assistant professor will have a provisional review at three years, and a full review including at least six arms length outside expert candidate assessments after six years. The possible outcomes are to be granted tenure and promotion to associate professor, or to be rejected for tenure and fired. There is no second chance at the same university, and the arc of an individual's career is forever marked by this outcome.

The competitiveness of both professional golf and academic tenure as well as the high-profile and public judgments of value in each (the cut after two days in a tournament; getting tenure or getting fired) leads to a similar sense of self-reliance and focus on one's career. Faculty pursue their intellectual passions and are most rewarded for expertise in a narrow topical area. Professional golfers must hone their golf game and manage the travel realities of a touring professional in an idiosyncratic manner. Faculty are often guilty of "looking through" staff assistants, audiovisual technicians and information technology professionals daily, but faculty can erupt in self-righteous anger when something goes wrong once a semester. A working IT system, secure data storage, and people who clean offices all contribute to the success of faculty, but we are commonly unaware or forget to acknowledge or thank them. Professional golfers play only for themselves. However, a golf tournament requires hundreds of volunteers to create and support the workplace of pro golfers. For example, my wife volunteers annually as a gallery control person at a tournament, a ten hour-a day job for a week each year. This requires her to take a week of vacation from her job and she pays $150 for the shirt provided to her and the opportunity to volunteer. Professional golfers get courtesy cars, free food, and drinks in the clubhouse and on the course. The members of the host club where tournaments are held cannot play for several weeks.

Both professions are individualistic and competitive as well as dependent on the labor of others to make their success possible. This breeds in each a sense of self-reliance and resentment when someone tells them how they should do their job. And it puts both at great risk of forgetting all the people who make their career success possible.

Why Mass Produced DEI Won't Work for Faculty

The reality is that faculty are the largest purveyors *per capita* of racial harm at Duke, because we have such outsized power, and understand ourselves to be enlightened, and incapable of such bias. This is a blind spot that keeps us from seeing racism in its many forms, in ourselves. The problem is real and important, and how to fix it is unclear, but I believe the faculty will have to address this issue amongst ourselves, as a profession.

The most effective intervention against racism at Duke is for faculty to speak up when we see bias displayed in our daily, shared work. Faculty have the best chance to connect and convince faculty, be it about Racism or anything else, because we spend so much time together and are members of the same club and "in the room where it happens." We engage in direct conversation with one another in our research fields where new ideas and debate are expected, and we understand disciplinary evidence standards. This means that we are experienced and comfortable in determining when and how to change our minds, based on evidence. We are used to being critiqued, pushed, and questioned in our area of scholarly expertise, but have trouble with pushback in other areas of life. Most of us would be aghast if someone said that we were a racist, or that we were doing something racist. We are the only ones who can call each other out in a way that has a chance of resulting in true change.

An example of how we faculty can best connect with and convince faculty. I had a drink with several faculty colleagues after work in January 2020, and we were talking about the looming presidential election and the discussion turned to who would win the Democratic primary. Everyone present was a reliable liberal or progressive voter, and the talk that evening was who could defeat President Donald Trump, who we understood to be either unfit, dangerous, crazy or an amalgam of all of these. We focused on electability of the various Democratic candidates and the upcoming South Carolina primary, the first one in a Southern state that would feature a large proportion of Black voters. This was considered a test of who among the Democratic candidates could pull together an historically reliable voting bloc for the party in the general election. As the conversation flowed, one of my colleagues said,

"Blacks will always support Democrats because they will give them things like Medicaid expansion."

I study health policy, so I brought up the fact that in North Carolina, there were two White beneficiaries in the Medicaid program for each Black person so insured. This fact was noted with some surprise, but it is just a case of basic math. A higher rate of Medicaid eligibility among Black residents (which there is) among a group that comprises 22 percent of the population will be smaller in absolute terms than a slightly lower rate of the much larger group. Basic demography lesson done, the discussion quickly moved on, but unbeknownst to me, a seed had been planted. And it germinated.

About one month later, one of these colleagues came to my office and said that he had been struck by the point I made in our conversation, yet he realized when he heard the word "Medicaid" he thought of someone who was Black. He meant that if he closed his eyes and thought about Medicaid, he saw a Black person. Health policy is not his topic of expertise, so he had never thought much about health insurance. He viewed much of the opposition to the presidency of Barack Obama as racially motivated, including the reticence of North Carolina to expand the program as part of Obamacare. Now he saw himself as holding a racist idea himself in the simplest term of the word—Medicaid equaled Black in his mind's eye in spite of there being more White beneficiaries.

We talked about blind spots and how to respond when we discover them in ourselves and others. The visual aspects of Racism that are activated by the brain's perception of skin color, and the simple reality that faculty bring our perceptions and biases, strengths, and weaknesses with us to campus each day. We agreed that we need to work harder to understand how they affect us as teachers, researchers, and colleagues at Duke University. He had arrived at a crucial understanding about himself, one that I affirmed by acknowledging it in myself. Rejecting racism and seeing it in many places, ways, and people does not mean that you (me!) are exempt from also nurturing racist views and undertaking or supporting actions that result in racial harm. This is all true regardless of our intent, beliefs and how we vote. Because faculty have such outsized power on campus, small changes in our self-awareness and behavior can greatly improve the campus culture and the life of others. Via search committees, curriculum reviews, in research team meetings, and so on.

Faculty are simply human beings who have chosen a career that emphasizes following individual passions and interests and elevates discovery of new ideas and knowledge in narrow realms as the ultimate measure of value. Indeed, this is the point of a research university. Some parts of society are set aside to seek focused knowledge, some of which may seem esoteric and tangential to human experience at a given time, but that may one day provide an answer or insight of supreme importance. The work of the research university is super important, but so too are the people working there. Changes that are motivated by self-discovery can be powerful forces for good on campus. How could we make such self-discovery more common among the faculty at Duke? This is a question that continues to echo in my brain.

All mandated training is not bad. I experienced an implicit bias training that helped a hiring committee I chaired a decade ago deal with a difficult issue during our deliberations. Any department that wished to undertake a national search for a tenured, or tenure track faculty spot at that time had to ensure the committee completed a ninety-minute group training session that discussed bias in hiring and group decision-making. This requirement followed the adoption of one recommendation of the 2014 Academic Council Committee on Diversity and Bias on which I served. This 2014 committee was unusual because it was created by the faculty and not in response to a high-profile incident. It serves as a good example of faculty and administration working together to make Duke a more just workplace outside of the public view.

When it was time to complete the training by the search committee I chaired, there was the typical grumbling at having to attend any sort of faculty meeting or training. One faculty member in particular said that they had been a part of hiring for several decades and did not need a staff member from the provost's office to train them on how to do so. However, the members were told that to serve on the committee they had to participate in the training, and if they were unwilling to do so, they had to step aside. Everyone who was invited to serve on the committee participated in the training and we got to the crucial work of refreshing the ranks of our faculty.

The content of the training is not memorable, but it provided a shared experience that the committee later used to work through a conflict. We were later stuck in a disagreement when one of the committee members reminded us of a strategy that we learned in the training together, and we went through a quick exercise that de-escalated rising tension in the group and helped us to refocus on our task of hiring junior faculty.

Each committee member wrote their understanding of the issue at the heart of the dispute on a note card, and on the other side wrote what each member believed other members of the committee thought was going on. This exercise was eye opening. In five minutes, it demonstrated that we had not fully understood the position of our colleagues and it helped us to recalibrate, negotiate and complete our work. The quick exercise disrupted an escalating tension thus helping us put aside our opinions and return to the corporate nature of the work that we needed to complete. We had been directed by the department and the university to identify new members of the faculty and were not there to simply represent our own narrow intellectual interests. This was an example of training that had been imposed upon the group being useful because it provided us with shared experience that was focused on the corporate nature of the job we had to do together. Further, it shows the value of a search committee doing training together as opposed to only the chair doing so. The shared nature of the training was far more important than the details of the content of the training because it helped to orient us into a group that was completing an important task on behalf of others. And we managed to rise to the occasion.

Another intervention that has been used with mixed success is adding a university official from a Diversity office of some sort to a search committee. The logic of doing so acknowledges the small group nature of hiring committees, even though searches for a position like president, on which I served in 2016, can have fifteen to twenty members. Having a committee member in the room focus on process, fairness and following the institution's search guidelines allows for deviations to be nipped in the bud. This may stop certain types of discriminatory behavior, but shared training is more effective in my experience. Further, even if a faculty member holds the job of diversity officer or similar, many faculty will view them as having gone over "to the administrative" side and will view their input with skepticism.

I served in 2011 and 2012 on a negotiated rulemaking committee that was hosted by the Federal Department of Health and Human Services that illustrated how outside influence may not effectively alter committee deliberations. Rulemaking is the process of translating legislation into detailed rules of implementation. Laws tend to be general and may focus on goals or intent, and when there is ambiguity of how to implement a law, the Negotiated Rulemaking Act of 1986 provides for a structure to determine a consensus. A key part of rulemaking is its public nature. Agendas, reports, deliberations, and votes are all public and the sessions are recorded. A transcript is made and shared publicly. This is designed prevent bias from unfairly influencing negotiations and is based on the idea of "sunshine" laws that mandate transparency. And in my experience on this committee, it meant that most of the deals were cut in the bathroom during breaks. The point for the purpose of this book is that the best hope of changing faculty behavior lies with other faculty.

I began a project in 2021, with funding from Duke's provost office, to develop several research-based scenarios that could be used to stimulate faculty-only discussions of racism. The goal was to see if we could develop scenarios and vignettes that flowed from historical and archival research that could stimulate faculty-to-faculty discussion and a better understanding of how we might be contributing to negative aspects of the campus climate. The impetus to undertake this research was a training session I did during late summer, 2020, with several other faculty as part of a test run of some of Duke's newly minted anti-racist training sessions that flowed from the President's declaration in June. The number of participants who reached out to complain to me about the juvenile nature of the training was large. And I thought that they were more right than wrong. I fully supported President Price's call to change the culture of Duke, but felt that the faculty would have to figure out a way to heal ourselves, so to speak. The ideal outcome is to have faculty in small groups discussing issues and discovering our own hidden biases, racial and otherwise. A good example is the Medicaid conversation noted earlier, but that event was fully serendipitous, and the "intervention" that I made was tiny. But that is what change will look like. Could we develop tools to encourage this type of interaction?

In short, maybe.

The vulnerability and comfort that my small group of faculty friends shared in January 2020 is impossible to create on command during a training program's forty-five-minute session. However, if the university mandates that some type of training will be provided, trainings developed by and for the faculty might be viewed more positively by the professoriate. I got a grant to develop three such prompts and one worked well, one flopped and one was in between. The most meaningful prompt focused on examples of university-sanctioned racism at Duke. The university developed 300 home sites in the Duke Forest from 1931 to 1964 that had racially restrictive covenants embedded in the home deeds. Duke University imposed the racial covenants by choice and did so because they felt to recruit an excellent faculty to a university in the American South, they would have to provide a living situation that was insulated from people who were Black. I owned one such home and was shocked when I bought it in 2006 and read in the deed language that "no one of the Negro race" could sleep in the house unless they worked for me as a servant. Duke University included further language in the deeds that identified a process for removing such language that made such a change practically impossible. When I bought my house in 2006, there was a bright orange slip of paper stapled to this part of the deed that noted that this stipulation was unenforceable under federal law and had been for some time. So why was it still in the deed? There is a long, legal story that is somewhat unsatisfying, but for me the biggest issue was that Duke University had never fully come clean about why the university did it, how they did it, and what impact this history has on the campus and Durham today.

The discussion sessions I facilitated to test the interventions were idiosyncratic and unsurprisingly driven by who participated and how they choose to do so. Some faculty largely held back, did not say much, and stuck with discussing the history and public policy implications of residential segregation that has been imposed by a variety of means. This was familiar territory, and while some faculty were experts, the discussion did not hit too close to home for most participants. The sessions in which there was disagreement, challenge, and even a bit of vitriol of the how-dare-you variety, were better discussions and more useful. They had a chance of initiating a durable change. Differences in understanding became clear and we created a shared experience that members of the gathered faculty could recall later, for the good. Sometimes a faculty member would say they had thought of some aspect of our current discussion of racism at Duke and in the United States in a different way, at a slightly different angle than before. At other sessions, faculty thought that seeking to link these events was a waste of time. But we were talking. Training that gets faculty talking has the best chance of leading to meaningful change, in an area where any such change is difficult.

I am not optimistic about mass produced training to address racism among faculty members. On balance, it may make things worse. Shared training in group skills among search committees where tools are provided and the law and regulations of the university about discrimination are reinforced can be useful and is where our training efforts for faculty should focus.

CHAPTER NINE: DEI ROUND TRIP

The dream of reason did not take power into account

PAUL STARR IN THE SOCIAL TRANSFORMATION OF AMERICAN MEDICINE

I received a "trading round trip" warning in January, 2025 when initiating a 403-B retirement account change—I had not stayed long enough in a mutual fund and shifting in and out too quickly is bad for long term results, not only for me, but for everyone in the fund. There are parallels to the embrace, push back and rejection of DEI on university campuses and in Fortune 500 companies from 2017-2024.

The *Chronicle of Higher Education* is a daily publication read by many faculty and academic leaders that covers important topics in higher education and provides a good barometer of this pendulum swing in higher education. By the end of the first COVID summer of 2020 and into 2021, there was an explosion of new DEI positions, training conferences, online enrichment opportunities, and consultants prepared to shepherd campuses to their pledges of change. DEI was the new normal on campus and in the corporate boardroom. However, by the Fall of 2023, the *Chronicle of Higher Education* began publishing a new section entitled, "The Assault on DEI." This included a section that tracked state legislation designed to roll back the DEI advance, and there are numerous stories in the *Chronicle* of universities in 2023 and 2024 dismantling some or all of the DEI infrastructure that they so proudly created just a few years earlier. In states like Texas, Florida, and Iowa, legislatures and governing boards passed laws and internal university system resolutions were adopted that required such dismantling explicitly, or they were targeted financially within the budget process. Most corporations quietly moved on and changed the subject.

The catalyst for the sea-change was the U.S. Supreme Court's decision in June 2023 ruling that Harvard and UNC Chapel Hill's use of race-based affirmative action in undergraduate admissions was unconstitutional. This decision upended half a century of practice since the 1978 Bakke Supreme Court decision declared that diversity in education was a compelling interest of the nation, and therefore something legitimate and important for universities to foster via admissions policy. No more. The early equilibrium at Duke and most elite private universities was to collect demographic information including race in admissions, in part because of numerous federal laws that required its collection, but to end the use of explicit or formulaic weights for race in an admissions decision. President Vince Price made a statement following the ruling noting the continuing commitment of Duke University to recruit a diverse student body as well as its pledge to comply with the law. My alma mater, UNC Chapel Hill, one of the defendants in the Supreme Court case, made similar statements. However, the Board of Governors of the University of North Carolina System, in late July 2023, went even further than required by the decision and banned the use of race in college application essays, over the objections of at least one board member who said the UNC system should not go beyond what the Supreme Court had ruled. The entire board is dominated by Republicans and conservatives, and has been for the past decade or so, and some did not think the decision went far enough to end all of the race-conscious policies on campus, such as student affinity group centers.

Whether race can be used in admissions is irrelevant for most colleges and universities because there are less than fifty institutions in the United States that admit fewer than half of their applicants. A bigger challenge for most institutions of higher education is filling class rosters to keep them viable as ongoing business entities. At Duke, less than 5 percent of undergraduate applicants were admitted to the class of 2029, so minute shifts in policy could change the admit line a bit one way or another. So much attention was paid to the 2023 Supreme Court decision due to the outsize role of elite universities in credentialing, and the fact that there were numerous voices who wanted to go much further than simply banning the use of race in admissions. The Summer of 2023 was like a follow-on temblor just three years after the COVID earthquake upended higher education.

By 2024, policy changes well beyond those required by the Supreme Court decision had spread to North Carolina and the seventeen campuses of its public university system. The University of North Carolina Board of Governors ended campus-specific DEI goals and began to end certain jobs on specific campuses and to eradicate units. Many private businesses that led the way in new DEI initiatives in 2020 quietly walked back goals and commitments and eliminated jobs that focused on DEI. What was viewed as a key business strategy was dumped as it came to be seen as a potential liability to the bottom line. All of these trends accelerated as the nation hurtled toward the 2024 Presidential election, and the election of Donald Trump for the second time.

Since January 20, 2025, the Trump Administration has made anti-DEI rhetoric and policy follow through a hallmark of their early efforts, including firing generals who the President said were DEI hires, ending DEI training in the military, and deleting an executive order in force since 1965 that required private businesses who seek contracts with the federal government to not engage in racial discrimination. In the higher education realm, the

Trump Administration froze the NIH review process, imposed a new plan for how the federal government would pay university research infrastructure costs that is now being litigated, and began canceling *existing NIH grants* that do not align with the administrations priorities, many of them due to being labelled as DEI-infused projects. This was an unprecedented step that did not allow faculty to follow normal channels of remediation, because the government said the projects were irredeemable. On February 14, 2025 the Trump Administration issued a 'Dear Colleague' letterto colleges and universities that laid out aggressive plans to target race-conscious policies as violations of title 6, and then made an example of Columbia University by freezing under threat of cancellation $400 Million in federal grants due to the governments finding of widespread antisemitism on campus and inadequate efforts to combat same. It was quite a rapid round trip from DEI as the new normal societal commitment, to a political punching bag that became a short-hand slur, used by critics of higher education. Public universities were most directly affected by the sea change before the 2024 election, but private universities with large endowments like Columbia, Harvard, Princeton, Penn and Duke are squarely in the crosshairs at the end of March 2025 as this book is being completed. There are many attacks on higher education from outside our walls, but I want to finish by looking inward, to better understand our role in the DEI round trip.

*****

On June 17, 2020 Duke President Vince Price declared the institution's commitment to developing an anti-racist culture. He wrote in a letter to the Duke community and said, in part:

"In recognition of Juneteenth's message of liberation from oppression, and out of respect for the anger, sadness, exhaustion, and courage of our Black friends and neighbors, this Friday, June 19, will be a day of reflection for the entire Duke University community. I encourage you to pause from your regular work and reflect both on the ongoing history of systemic racial injustice and how it manifests in our neighborhoods, our places of work, our families, our faith communities, and at Duke. To the extent possible, managers should provide employees with time to take part in programs and observances for this day of memory and contemplation.

I hope that this opportunity for reflection will prove valuable for you, as I know it will for me. I cannot as a white person begin to fully understand the daily fear and pain and oppression that is endemic to the Black experience. Instead, I have been seeking to listen, and to learn. I've been meeting with my colleagues and reading Black authors and theorists, some here at Duke. And I've been reflecting on our national, and regional, and institutional history."

This was a bold statement that I am confident was heartfelt and came from a place of personal growth for President Price, but it was also stunning from an institutional perspective. I don't think it was performative on his part, but I do believe that he made a crucial error in beginning something of this magnitude without having the faculty of the university on board. Particularly those whose research expertise was in relevant areas.

I was energized by the announcement and surprised by how cautious and uncertain some of the Duke faculty were whose research expertise focused on studying aspects of race or racism. The ones I spoke with were immediately cautious, even worried. How would Duke ever match the bold language with action? And how was the campus, exhausted by the transitions brought on by COVID, going to have the bandwidth to follow through on this culture change given his insistence that we had to act fast?

Faculty leaders began calling me and asking if I knew this was coming since I am a former Chair of the Academic Council at Duke and have been around the Gothic Wonderland since Dinosaurs roamed the Earth—no, I did not and was surprised by the President's boldness. Most surprisingly, none of my faculty friends and colleagues who were Black and in leadership positions, and/or whose research expertise included race in some manner knew of this plan, nor had they been involved in developing it, and the language used. And some of them were immediately worried, even as they acknowledged the bold leadership and appreciated the intent. As one said to me:

"I don't know what anti-racism means."

Language is always important, especially to academics who parse things for a living. Anti-racism flowed directly from a 2019 book by Ibram Kendi entitled *"How to be an antiracist"* and the dichotomous division of all things into racist or not proved to be an unstable base of action for a University-wide culture change. I am fully confident that declaring Juneteenth a Duke holiday to first be observed two days later and committing us to an anti-racist culture was an earnest and heartfelt expression of what President Price understood to be best for the university community at that time, but well intentioned does not equal well executed, nor does it make it a good idea.

******

A few weeks before in early June, 2020, I made one of the biggest mistakes of my leadership career at Duke University when I called three meetings for employees of the Social Science Research Institute (SSRI) that I directed from July 1, 2019- December 31, 2024: one for individuals who identified as Black; one for those who were White; and an "all hands" meeting. A portion of my email text is below:

"The last few months, and now the last few days, have been the most tumultuous times the United States has seen in the past fifty years. I would like to provide an opportunity for SSRI staff to check in with me via Zoom if you wish to do so. I want to first hold a session with our colleagues who are Black—the disproportionate burden of the COVID pandemic on the Black community along with the killing of several Black men over the past few weeks culminating with Mr. Floyd's killing and the protest, police response, and subsequent rioting has this nation on a knife's edge. The logic of my first meeting with our Black colleagues simply acknowledges the disproportionate nature of the harm that is and has been experienced."

My email provides a case study in the difference between intent and effect. Looking back, my primary error was responding emotionally without running my plan by others whom I trusted and who knew me well and the context of SSRI and Duke. I was in too much of a rush to lead, to do.... *something*. My short email is packed with mistakes, and it probably made things worse.

First, several staff members and faculty felt excluded from the discussion—they identified as neither Black nor White. They were correct, I had excluded them. Duke is a global university that combines the 400-year Black/White legacy that is a unique product of chattel slavery in the United States, with numerous racial, ethnic, and national identities on campus that makes the community far more complex than the Black/White dichotomy that I learned growing up and that has been reinforced in my adult life. I continue to struggle to break out of organizing my thinking along a racial binary.

Second, several staff wondered how I constructed a list of "the Black staff" and "the White staff," and this made them fearful. Why was the director of the institute creating lists of SSRI staff and affiliates that were stratified by race? This was an understandable feeling that in retrospect I should have foreseen. The meeting announcements were sent to the same email address group. If I were going to have segregated meetings, I should have stated that individuals were to self-identify into them. What made things worse was that I sent the message as a bcc so that recipients could not tell who else had received this email and while I think that is good email hygiene generally, it increased anxiety in this context.

Third, there were a few staff on the White only Zoom

discussion who felt that I was inappropriately forceful in some of my language, and one who later told me they felt that I was being racist toward White people. Push back of this type is common across U.S. history when there has been any sort of progress made in racial terms. It's to be expected. However, the leader of an organization must be mindful of their relative power when calling a meeting that addresses a topic that many consider to be political, intimidating, and scary. I had not been and that was a mistake. I had abused my power, perhaps to make me feel better about myself that at least I was *trying to do something*.

That was a lot of mistakes in one short email, regardless of my intent. I had a lot of apologizing and listening to do.

****

Looking back on my past seven years in leadership at Duke, I would gladly trade all DEI programming (useful workshops, wastes of time, everything in between) for a more fully taught U.S. history in school, and a lifelong conversation about how history affects us all today. We need more discussion, interpretation, debate and disagreement, not less. Let me provide an example of what I mean.

The most famous person from my hometown of Goldsboro, N.C. is Charles B. Aycock, a lawyer born in 1859 who became Governor of North Carolina from 1901-04. I briefly mentioned him earlier in this book. I visited his birthplace farm on several occasions growing up during school field trips and the like and knew him by the moniker the "Education Governor" whose statue was placed in the U.S. Capitol in 1932 and who was a namesake for a Democratic Party fundraiser, the Vance-Aycock Dinner until 2011.

One night in the late 1990s when I was a brand-new Assistant Professor, I listened to an author talking on the radio as I drove my sleeping family about a race riot and *coup d'etat* in Wilmington, NC in 1898. I was stunned. My first thought was what the hell was he talking about? I had never heard this story even though the port city was well known to me since Goldsboro High School played the three Wilmington schools in sports. I spent hours on a rickety activity bus driving to and from Wilmington to play football and golf. What really piqued my interest was when the author mentioned that Charles B. Aycock was involved in a series of speeches around the state fomenting White Supremacy with protection from the so-called Red Shirts from 1898-1900. Aycock helped create the context for the 1898 Wilmington coup. I have since come to learn that Aycock, a former United States Attorney by this time, was essentially a learned, and well-spoken front man for a racist mob.

The history taught at his birthplace in the 1970s and 1980s was sanitized. This is another way of saying that it was a lie based on what was left out of the telling. Today, the history provided at the Aycock birthplace and on the historic site's webpage contains a reasonable telling of the positions, views and history of the life of Governor Charles B. Aycock. An excerpt below:

"Born in rural Wayne County, Charles B. Aycock became the fiftieth Governor of North Carolina in 1901. While Aycock has been traditionally celebrated by citizens and state leaders alike for expanding public education and constructing over 1,000 schools while in office, less attention was given to his involvement with the Wilmington Massacre and Coup of 1898, the violent Red Shirt movement of 1898-1900, or the newspaper propaganda which contributed to his "White supremacy" campaign for governor in 1900. Today the site interprets his legacy as a supporter of education, a segregationist, and a driving force behind the disenfranchisement of Black North Carolinians."

During the 1900 gubernatorial campaign, Aycock focused on White rule and the goal of disenfranchising Black citizens who had gotten the right to vote after the passage of the 13th, 14th and 15th Amendments to the U.S. Constitution. As the soon-to-be Governor wrote in a letter to the editor of the *Alamance Gleaner* on June 28, 1900:

"In dealing with the question of eliminating the negro vote, I did say that I knew of but three ways in which a minority of whites could rule a majority of negroes - by force, by fraud, or by law."

Aycock was elected Governor at the same time the voters of the state passed an amendment to the North Carolina Constitution in 1900, that technically adhered to the Reconstruction Amendment prohibitions against denying the vote based on "race, color or previous condition of servitude" while still leading to mass disenfranchisement of Blacks. Instead, they added a literacy test that was unfairly applied, a poll tax and the use of a "grandfather" clause that served to expand voting among poor Whites (if your grandfather could vote, you could) while excluding Blacks (whose grandfather's would have been enslaved).

My home state invented grandfathering, to keep Black people from voting. Perhaps most bizarrely, the North Carolina Democratic Party did not remove Aycock's name from its Vance-Aycock dinner until 2011, when Barack Obama was President. Perhaps the most persistent reality of North Carolina politics the past 150 years is that one of the two major political parties has wanted to reduce the ability of Black folks to vote.

It really pisses me off that we were not taught a more complete history of Charles B. Aycock, and doing so is neither DEI nor critical race theory. It is US History.

North Carolina public schools teach a year-long unit in N.C. history in 4th and 8th grade. I have no idea what happened in 4th grade, but we learned none of this in 8th grade. Teenagers are certainly aware that no one is all good or all bad and they can handle and process not only the history of what took place, but how and why the version of history told has changed. Most importantly, we need to ask 14-year-olds what they think about our history and what it means for all of us today and tomorrow. We need to teach and discuss a more fully told U.S. history and learn to talk with one another about it. We won't always agree, but that is the point.

****

We faculty can be an unruly and chaotic bunch, and I have already mentioned that we are not great at pulling off conspiracies and that is because we view ourselves as the ultimate free agents. More beholden to a discipline, topic, research method or art form than to a given University. You want to see a group that believes in markets—it is faculty, who are always wondering if there is a better deal to be had at another University. The key question when evaluating any such deal is where a faculty member can most productively conduct their research, the professional task that is most important to us.

It is important to realize when discussing the arc of the DEI round trip at Duke that it was precisely the faculty with research expertise in race who were the ones who were uncertain about the practical meaning of anti-racism as a campus organizing principle when President Price used it to frame Duke University's response in June, 2020. Such faculty are commonly painted in negative light by critics of the university as crazy liberals, leaders of the "woke mob" on campus, or activists instead of scholars. However, their reticence born of the inherent academic conservatism was proven prescient, painting them in a more realistic light. They are scholars who have given their life's work to study race, and they were rightly skeptical of Duke's ability to engage in the desired change in such short order, especially when they, the experts, had not been consulted. The desire to move quickly and lead boldly is antithetical to engaging faculty on a difficult question, and the faculty with expertise must be front and center of anything important on campus if it is to work. If not, or if that is impossible, then it is not something that has any business being done by a university.

A few years later, during President Price's 2024 annual

address to the faculty, the phrase "anti-racist" cannot be found. His words on race and Duke were as follows:

We are deepening our commitments to racial and social equity, and I am very grateful for the continued work of the Racial Equity Advisory Council and the Offices of Institutional Equity and Faculty Advancement, which are driving this important initiative into its third year.

Duke is changing at the unit and local level, and we are making real progress toward fostering a more inclusive campus community. In January, over three hundred campus leaders participated in a day-long retreat focused on racial equity. It was a terrific program —led by Kim Hewitt, Abbas Benmamoun, and Sherrilyn Black, with contributors from dozens of units. Looking ahead, we are working toward the release of the "Duke Annual Report on Racial Equity" or the DARRE, which will help units track and measure their progress."

In the past two years, we've funded thirty-five faculty research projects supporting efforts to understand and address systemic racism, including 17 projects related to race, racism, and the history of the American South and 18 projects related to racial inequality.

The language moved on as the times changed, and the need to measure progress for a massive organization became increasingly important. And a lot of work. The colleagues leading these initiatives for Duke are great people, diligent workers and all friends who are giving their professional lives to make Duke a better place. If we are looking inward, I think that we need to have fewer initiatives that are outside of our research and teaching, and to ensure that the faculty are vitally involved in all of them.

The resources made available by President Price noted above have enabled research that might otherwise not have been done, facilitating the faculty doing their work. This support is much appreciated. And that is the point of the university. In fact, I lead a team of researchers that included several undergraduate students in an archival look at the role of racially segregated health care at Duke University from 1930-70 using resources made possible by President Price's initiative to change Duke's culture.

We found a fascinating story underneath the basic facts of Duke hospital providing care in segregated medical wards and clinics, which is well-known and simply the state of the world in the 1930s American South. However, I had heard the story told as the segregated wards developing based on patient preferences and agreed to by leaders of Duke only under their pressure, but that is not the case. In Duke's archives we found planning documents that clearly noted segregated wards being planned prior to construction—maternity ward White; maternity ward Negro—and so on.

When Duke University Hospital opened on July 9, 1930, treating White and Negro patients albeit in segregated wards, this was progressive for the time. Locally, both the White hospital (Watts) and the Negro hospital (Lincoln) were worried about the competition for their patient population, and the leaders of Watts feared pressure to someday treat Negros, and that of course did come in 1964 (Civil Rights Act) and 1965 (creation of Medicare and Medicaid). The hospital associated with Wake Forest School of Medicine down the road in Winston-Salem, NC did not treat any Black patients until the early 1960s, at which point Duke had been doing so for three decades. However, the reality of Duke's health care history is that generations of Black Durham NC residents have experienced separate and not equal care in a variety of ways provided by Duke, partly explaining at least some of the ubiquitous Duke machinations about why the community does not trust us more given how many jobs in Durham that we provide.

Our history has much to teach about tomorrow if we will listen to one another.

The image below is a photograph of a wall mural from the bowels of the oldest part of the Duke Medical Center depicting Carl Rogers, a Black man who was the right hand staff member of the founding Dean of the Duke School of Medicine, Wilburt Davison, as *Thomas* the Tank Engine. Dean Davison, who was a Pediatrician, is depicted as the conductor and two prominent Pediatricians are riding in the Caboose. Dean Davison referred to Carl Rogers as the Assistant Dean of the School of Medicine, and his papers in the archives are filled with references to the many things they did together at Duke (figure used with permission of Duke University Medical Archives).

I have shown this photograph during numerous talks and in classes at Duke and the huge variations in reaction are fascinating. From 'this is honoring Carl Rogers' to 'this is demeaning to him', and everything in between. The best part about showing this image is that it gets people talking and listening to one another. Especially when they find out that this was on a wall in the Duke School of Medicine from sometime in the early 1950s until 2018 when it was removed, for reasons that are unclear to me (it is difficult to see, but someone had etched 'White' across the

Caboose, but nothing else appears to have been written on the mural). Someone thought of calling the University Medical Center Archives to come and document the removal of a mural and the creation of an artifact. We are still trying to better understand why this was done.

I loved the process of this archival project. Losing myself for hours in the archives, leafing through letters, notes, reports and often forgetting why I had opened a box in the first place. However, the best thing about this project was seeing the look of discovery on one of the undergraduate team members' face when she told me that a document she found seemed to prove that segregated wards were planned ahead of time and did not develop due to patient pressures. *She had experienced the joy of discovery.*

It was such a great moment.

What I love most about my job is the *process* of research, especially when conducted with a team that can discuss and debate what new pieces of evidence mean. Every answer produces ten more questions, and it never stops. Learning never stops so long as we remain human, which most fundamentally means that we are capable of changing our mind. Higher Education is under attack for some good and many bad reasons and it is unclear what comes next. I think we need to get back to basics and to remember why we became scholars. Why we have given our lives to research and teaching. To recall the true North of higher education—so long as there are faculty, students and some books, you can have a university.

CHAPTER TEN: WHY ARE YOU SO OBSESSED WITH RACE?

Obsession is the wellspring of genius and madness

MICHEL DE MONTAIGNE

Some folks have asked me recently 'why are you so obsessed with race?' It is a fair question, and the simplest answer is that I have come to understand the American obsession with race, from the beginning of the nation, and how that has affected my life and our shared future. Race encapsulates the idea that some are worth more than others. I have said a few times in this volume that race has been the most consistently powerful idea to influence my life from growing up in Eastern North Carolina to being a faculty leader at Duke University. And the elevation of race was a choice born from the clash of two other ideas: equality and hierarchy. The Declaration of Independence announced the United States as the beautiful idea of equality, one that remains worth seeking even as we have come so far.

"We hold these truths to be self-evident, that all men are created equal, that they are endowed by their Creator, with certain unalienable rights, that among these are Life, Liberty and the pursuit of Happiness."

However, this idea ran head long into another just eleven years later in Article 1, Section 2, Clause 3 of the U.S. Constitution, the so-called "three-fifths compromise" that provided a formula for exactly how people were unequal for the purposes of determining the size of the population, and therefore the amount of taxation and the apportionment of political representation to each state.

"Representatives and direct Taxes shall be apportioned among the several States which may be included within this Union, according to their respective Numbers, which shall be determined by adding to the whole Number of free People, including those bound to Service for a Term of Years, and excluding Indians not taxed, three-fifths of all other People. The actual Enumeration shall be made within three Years after the first Meeting of the Congress of the United States, and within every subsequent Term of ten Years, in such Manner as they shall by law direct...."

The Constitution defined the nation as an amalgam of equality and hierarchy, knit together via compromise to form a union around chattel slavery, whose impact on US history is profound and well known. A civil war was required to end it, and the nation and campus still struggle to come to grips with its effects on society today. We still debate whether the lead General who lost the civil war should be honored on campus, after all. Or whether the road from Sanford, NC to Pinehurst, NC should continue to be named the Jefferson Davis highway, in honor of the political leader of the Confederacy. However, what I have come to understand is that the original sin of the United States was not slavery, but race. Let me explain what I mean.

The United States had a *chance at a race-free society in spite of Slavery* in 1790, if we had simply collected the two demographic variables that were required to comply with the Constitution for the purpose of determining population size for political representation and taxation: (1) male or female; (2) slave or free. The following clause from the 1790 Census Act is one of the most consequential in US history, , "... *distinguishing also the sexes and colours of free people* ..."

The first U.S. Congress did not think that slave and free was enough detail. They elevated race as an American idea by choice and preference. The Congress chose to divide *free people* by race, even though they did not do the same for those who were enslaved. Instead, of the required binary, the Census Act of 1790 mandated the following categorization: (1) slaves; (2) free white females and males; (3) all other free people. The father of the nation, George Washington, signed the Census Act into law, and the writer of the Declaration of Independence, then Secretary of State Thomas Jefferson, oversaw the implementation of the first census count. This reality was not obvious to me until the last few years.

The idea of race gave birth to Black Code laws passed in 1866 in North Carolina. The goal was to transfer as many limitations from slavery to people who were not White as possible, in direct opposition to what the nation said we would do in the reconstruction Amendments to the Constitution. If you doubt the extension of the legacy of slavery via the language of race, go read the Civil Rights Acts of 1866 and 1964 and reflect on why such similar laws were required nearly a century apart?

White liberals and progressives like me wanted to believe that we had moved past the legacy of race in our history with the election of Barack Obama as president. His election was a tremendous step, but my assumptions about what it meant were an ahistorical delusion. The errors and assumptions that I and we made at Duke greatly influenced the campus that we find today. One that is not filled with the open dialogue and debate that we want and need on college campuses. President Obama's election coincided with Duke's expansion of need based financial aid, two things that happened simultaneously, but that had no other linkage, save fate. Duke's investment of huge sums of money into need based financial aid resulted in a wonderfully diverse student body based on family income and wealth, race, religion, and nation of origin. However, we were too busy congratulating ourselves for success in that effort to think about whether we might need to revise our methods of assimilating new students to our campus culture. And to be clear about exactly what exactly we were inviting them to join.

We did and we do.

A university is most fundamentally, the clash of two ideas: equality and hierarchy. Just like the United States. Equality in the sense that any question can be posed and answered, but hierarchy in that all answers are not equally valid. The university exists to seek the truth. If you are willing to take responsibility for your words, describe your methods, and divulge your findings or propositions in a manner that allows scrutiny and debate, you are welcome to join the intellectual fray of the campus. But, if you do so, your claims will be subjected to scrutiny, and you will have to make the case. The disciplines have methods of procedure and rules for judging the validity of claims, which is another way of saying that they have rules that govern how they disagree and fight. An openness to any question being posed because it will be judged by evidence, allows scholars to move toward the truth and expand knowledge. Telling a scholar that their theory has not been validated because there is not enough statistical evidence to reject the null hypothesis of no effect is not canceling them. It is the very functioning of the university and the primary reason the institution exists.

Racism of all types is anathema to this type of reasoned debate, and is the wrongful assignment of attributes to a person or group based on faulty evidence, lack of reasoning or deep seated prejudice. The persistence of the idea that some are worth more than others unfortunately lingers and it can only be defanged by our learning to talk about it so that we can better understand one another's experience. Let me provide an example.

When my friend and colleague Professor Kerry Haynie, became Dean of Social Sciences at Duke University on July 1, 2022, he moved into an office overlooking the beautiful Gothic quad where throngs of students passed each day. The Allen Building is synonymous with power and prestige at Duke because that is where the president, provost, and deans work each day. As the staff oriented him to his new office, he did something that would have never crossed my mind because he is Black and I am White. Upon being shown a panic button under his desk that would summon campus police, Dean Haynie wanted his picture provided to the Duke police department so that they would know that a Black man was the Dean of Social Sciences. Professor Haynie recounted this story to me over a drink after a round of golf a week later and said that he did not want the campus police responding to an emergency and "shooting me because I am Black," based on the assumption that he did not belong in that space. His life experience taught him that if there was trouble, most people who came upon it would assume that it must be the Black guy causing it. My life experience has not taught me such worries.

Professor Haynie's identity as a Black man is something that he has been aware of most of his life, while I never thought much about being White as an identity until the last decade. I viewed being White as a fact. Other people had identities; I saw myself as simply me. A basic reality of my blessed life has been that in most places that I have ever been or aspired to go in the United States, it was not unusual to see a White man, and so there were no second looks or worse. There is a tremendous benefit of reduced stress, and not having to deal with the type of worry that led Professor Haynie to let the police know that he was the new Dean of Social Sciences.

Dean Haynie's fear that the Duke police might mistake him for the troublemaker is based in the historical reality of White as the preferred, the baseline, the holder of power first enacted in the 1790 Census. And the only Census category that has persisted in all 23 Census counts, unchanged, is White. At Duke and other college campuses, the idea that some are worth more than others plays out in many forms: anti-Semitism, anti-immigrant sentiment, anti- Asian bias, the assumption that Muslims are terrorists, religious bigotry, ideas that those from Appalachia and the rural South are dense, and so on. We have a wonderfully diverse student body, and they all must deal with many forms of illegitimate hierarchy on a campus where we claim equality to rule. The primary reason to continue to address racism at Duke is because it is inconsistent with what we as an intellectual community say about ourselves—that we are scholars who proceed based on open dialogue, debate and rules of evidence. Racism in all its forms is the antithesis. And the search for the truth is why the university exists.

The most basic thing that I learned from 2017-2024 while serving in two leadership posts at Duke is that ideas are powerful and persistent, and that one must be replaced by another to be defeated. The idea of equality remains worth pursuit, and our route forward runs through our past as we learn to talk more openly about the scourge of bigotry of all types. Long journeys are hard, and we need each other along the way. Take my hand, let's go together.

WORKS MENTIONED

Beyer, Adam, and Sarah Kerman. 2018. "Group of Students Protest President Price's Alumni Address, Issue Demands." *The Duke Chronicle*, April 14.

Brownell, Kelly, and Linda Burton. 2016. *Task Force on Bias and Hate Releases Report.* May 4. Accessed May 1, 2024. https://today.duke.edu/2016/05/taskforcereport.

Christensen, Rob. 2018. "Profs Ignore Duke's Past to Shun Carr." *News and Observer.* Raleigh: McClathy, September 2.

Chronicle, Duke. 2024. "Survey of Faculty Political Beliefs." April 15.

Conover, Christopher C. 2017. "The case against Medicaid expansion." *North Carolina Medical Journal* 48-50.

CTSI, Duke. 2020. "Research Symposium-A Call to Action: Identifying Next Steps to Address Biomedical, Health Care, and Social Drivers of COVID-19 Disparities." May 22. Accessed May 2, 2024. https://ctsi.duke.edu/news/research-symposium-call-action-identifying-next-steps-address-biomedical-health-care-and.

History, Duke University Commission on Memory and. 2017. *Report: Commission on Memory and History.* Durham, November 17.

History, Duke University Department of. 2018. *Text of History Department Request on Building Name.* Durham, August 31.

Huler, Scott. 2023. "The Race Course." April 1. Accessed May 2, 2024. https://dukemag.duke.edu/collections/race-course.

Laconic, The Standard. 1967. "New Deputies Hired." *The Standard

Laconic, July 14.

Price, Vince. 2018. *President's Message on Vandalism at the Mary Lou Williams Center.* August 27. Accessed May 1, 2024. https://today.duke.edu/2018/08/presidents-message-vandalism-mary-lou-williams-center.

Price, Vincent. 2017. *Duke Today: Duke Removes Robert E. Lee Statue from Chapel Entrance.* Durham, August 19.

—. 2018. "President's Message on Duke Chapel Space." *Duke Today.* Durham: Duke University, August 16.

Schemmel, Alec. 2022. *Professor Refuses to Attend Mandatory DEI Training, Calls It Maoist Propaganda.* May 26. Accessed May 3, 2024. https://abcnews4.com/news/nation-world/professor-refuses-to-attend-mandatory-dei-training-calls-it-left-wing-maoist-propaganda.

Staddon, John. 2022. *Science in an Age of Unreason.* New York: Simon and Schuster.

Taylor Jr, Donald H. 2017. "The case for Medicaid expansion." *North Carolina Medical Journal* 43-47.

Taylor, Don. 2019. "Honor, Thank You, Unease: An Address from the Academic Council Chair." May 10. Accessed May 2, 2024. https://today.duke.edu/2019/05/honor-thank-you-unease-address-academic-council-chair.

—. 2019. "What is the problem with Duke? White Supremacy is the Root." *The Duke Chronicle*, August 22: 8.

University, Duke. 1969. *Protests, Pickets and Demonstrations.* Accessed May 1, 2024. https://policies.duke.edu/policy/pickets-protest-and-demonstrations/.

Wagner, Andrew. 2021. *Buried Monuments: The Legacy of Racial Covenants in Duke Forest.* Research Monograph, Durham: Self Published.

ABOUT THE AUTHOR

Donald H. Taylor, Jr.

Don Taylor is a professor of public policy at Duke, where he has been on the faculty since 1997. His research focuses on health policy, and he is currently working on a book project Renewing the Marketplace of Ideas on Elite College Campuses. He writes a substack on higher education reform called "Two Ditches" https://dontaylor13.substack.com/ where he focuses on academic freedom, the economics of elite higher education and the role of sports on campus.